21.95

S0-AXM-609

Man and Dog
The Psychology of a Relationship

Reinhold Bergler

HOWELL
BOOK HOUSE INC.

© 1988 by Professor R. Bergler

Published in North America 1989 by
Howell Book House Inc.
230 Park Avenue
New York, N.Y. 10169

Library of Congress
Cataloging-in-Publication Date

Bergler, Reinhold, 1929
    (Mensch und Hund. English)
    Man and dog: the psychology of a
    relationship/Reinhold Bergler.
      p. cm.
    Translation of: Mensch und Hund.
    Bibliography: p.
    ISBN 0-87605-688-5
    1. Dog owners – Psychology. 2. Dogs
    – Psychological aspects.
    3. Dogs – Therapeutic use.
    4. Human-animal relationships.
  I. Title.
  SF422.7.B4713 1988
  636.7'0019–dc19

All rights reserved. No part of this
publication may be reproduced, stored in a
retrieval system, or transmitted, in any form
or by any means, electronic, mechanical,
photocopying, recording, or otherwise
without the prior permission of the
copyright owner.

First published 1986 in Germany
  by Edition Agrippa

Photoset by Enset (Photosetting)
Midsomer Norton, Bath, Avon

Printed in Great Britain

Translated by Brian Rasmussen and Dana Loewy

Contents

Foreword   iv

1 Introduction   1

2 The role of the dog in art and culture   7

3 Dogs and personality   15

4 The role of dogs in prophylaxis and therapy   38

5 The role of dogs in developmental psychology   51

6 The psychology of dog ownership – experimental design principles   67

7 Results of the study   94

8 Positive psychological evaluation of dog ownership   108

9 Overall psychological evaluation of dog ownership   131

10 Preconceptions and prejudices: dogs and society   150

11 Psychological groups and types of dog owner   158

Concluding remarks   174

Appendix   175

References   180

Foreword

All life is essentially social in character. We live our lives in association with other people, animals, inanimate objects, values – everything, in fact, that goes to make up our 'environment'. Our quality of life and well-being are determined to a significant degree by the importance that we attach to other people and other things. Relationships between human beings and animals are an integral part of this world of meanings and values in which we live. This study is an attempt to examine the nature of these relationships, their potential significance and the effect they can have on our lives.

In preparing this study for publication, we were prevented by limitations of space from including all the data that were collected and processed in the course of our research. All calculations were performed on an IBM 3081 at the RH Computer Centre in Bonn.

Research is always the product of a dialogue. It can only thrive and flourish in the context of a co-operative endeavour that is both critical and creative. Academic status alone is no longer an adequate guarantee of authoritative, high-quality research. We should therefore like to take this opportunity of thanking all those people who assisted with the planning of this study, the analysis of the published scientific literature, the development of a methodology, the conduct of the field work, the analysis and processing of the data, the preparation of the manuscript and a critical reading of the completed text.

In particular, for their assistance and encouragement well beyond the call of duty, I should like to thank the following:

Ulrike Bolle, Dr E. Bruckert, Dr Katrin Harich, Dr Brigitte Höcke-Pörzgen, Dr H.-G. Hoff, Herr K. Kleinfeld, Dr Elena de Graat, Jutta Tschech.

Prof. R. Bergler

1 Introduction

Subjecting the self-evident to scientific scrutiny

Psychology is the study of human behaviour in all its myriad manifestations, from the ordinary and everyday to the pathological. As such it seeks to identify the inward causes of human behaviour, and aspires to enhance the quality of life and human well-being in the broadest sense through research, diagnosis and therapy. Its capacity for solving problems is evident in the contribution it makes to the description, elucidation, prediction and modification of human behaviour. Psychological studies must always take into account the religious, cultural, ecological and political factors that govern human behaviour, social interaction and behavioural habits. A psychology that only studies human behaviour under laboratory conditions, and then generalizes on the basis of these findings, cannot lay claim to scientific credibility or indeed to any practical social relevance.

Man is a social being, an entity in which knowledge and ignorance, hope and fear, love and hate, disappointment and triumph, loneliness and conflict, sympathy and antipathy, depression and joy are frequently – and paradoxically – intertwined. Man is thus exposed to a wide variety of stimuli, incentives and imperatives which impel him to interact with himself and other people, with cultural and religious structures, and with his environment in the broadest sense of the term. Since the dawn of mankind, animals have always played an important part in the complex scheme of human relationships. The history of mankind and the history of animals are by no means unconnected – quite the reverse. In fact, animals have always been influenced and changed in their development by humans – and vice versa.

The history of mankind has always been founded on the interdependence of human being, animals and nature in the general scheme of things. The course of that history has been shaped by the particular contemporary significance that animals have held for man in the past and, as we shall see, continue to hold for him in the present, albeit in somewhat modified forms. The essential unity of

1

man, nature and the animal kingdom has always been viewed as something self-evident and natural: an everyday fact of life.

If we confine our attention to domestic animals, it is easy to see that animals in this situation have always served as a source of help and support to man. They helped him to hunt more effectively, protected him against strangers and foes, eased the burden of physical labour and made it more efficient – and they also created an atmosphere of intimacy, security and companionship.

Man is a creature of many needs, who has always turned to dogs for protection, support, stimulation and delight. Man and animal, dog and master, have formed a natural partnership throughout long periods of human history. The essential characteristic of most natural relationships is that we take them for granted. We have ceased to be consciously aware of them, we do not generally give them much thought, and we do not talk about them. They simply exist, as if by some automatic mechanism. As long as man and dog formed such a natural, self-evident partnership they were not a matter for public debate – let alone a source of controversy, as they are in our own day.

Although human co-existence is to a very large extent determined and regulated by such self-evident phenomena, which also exercise a corrective and stabilizing function, psychological research has taken remarkably little note of them as long as they have remained self-evident – that is they have not been called into question by naive scepticism or scientific curiosity.

Self-evident or accepted modes of behaviour are ultimately an expression of cultural, religious and social rules and patterns of conduct, which are passed on quasi-automatically by tradition and education, constantly re-affirmed through example and underpinned by a system of rewards and punishments, and finally given society's seal of approval. In an earlier study of patterns of human hygiene and cleanliness I was able to show how different cultures have given rise to very different norms and patterns of behaviour, with corresponding differences in what is accepted as self-evident (see Bergler, 1974). The considerable differences in the purification rites that Buddhists and Christians practise in their daily lives, for example, have resulted in the creation of very different unconscious assumptions. Such unconscious assumptions – which also embrace habits and customs – have been widely ignored in experimental psychology and psychodiagnosis. This is primarily because we are dealing here with attitudes, patterns of behaviour and other variables that are shared by large numbers of people in all kinds of different situations – with abstracts, in short, that are ill-suited to define persons as individuals. Given their enormous importance for the regulation of human behaviour and as a key to human actions, the dearth of scientific studies in this field is an astonishing omission.

Accepted modes of behaviour possess neither absolute stability nor universal validity. In other words, 1. there are limits to the validity of accepted modes of behaviour, and 2. accepted modes of behaviour are subject to change.

1. *The limited validity of accepted modes of behaviour.* It is readily apparent even to the casual observer that there are big differences between different peoples and different cultures in terms of how people greet each other, how they relate to their more distant kin, how they celebrate Christmas or indeed any other festival, how they prepare certain types of food, what kind of dress is considered appropriate for certain occasions, what kind of animals are kept, how and in what numbers they are kept, etc. In the first instance, such accepted modes of behaviour apply only within certain specific groups, institutions, peoples or societies. At the same time – and this is a point that is often overlooked – it cannot be assumed that these more or less automatic modes of behaviour are condoned or practised by every member of a social group. While it is undoubtedly true that accepted modes of behaviour are always practised to a greater or lesser extent by the vast majority, there are always minorities who question such behaviour. Sometimes such minorities are vociferous in their demands for an alternative pattern of behaviour, which they themselves proceed to implement.

2. *Accepted modes of behaviour are subject to change.* While shared attitudes, convictions, rules of conduct and modes of behaviour are generally very stable, and often endure for many generations, gradual change – and in revolutionary periods even radical change – can and does occur. Under certain circumstances minority groups are in a position to influence, and ultimately change, the behaviour of the majority – as Moscovici has shown (1979). By opposing the slaughter of baby seals, a committed group of people has called into question the whole practice – formerly taken for granted – of processing and wearing a particular type of animal skin. In other words, they have brought about a change in consumer behaviour.

We are clearly living in an age when certain accepted modes of behaviour which are both desirable and popular are being called into question and threatened, not just by minority groups, but to an increasing extent by the so-called majority as well. It is also a fact that modes of behaviour that were once taken for granted are called into question and regarded as a suitable subject for research only to the extent that they have *ceased* to be taken for granted. A few examples will make this abundantly clear. We no longer assume that people will help each other out in emergencies or in cases of accident. It is no longer taken for granted that people can live together in an extended family situation feeling united and interdependent, but at the same time secure – nor that children will grow up in natural surroundings with a natural affinity for animals. Sadly, we can no longer assume that our forests will remain healthy, or that nature itself will go on endlessly supplying man's needs for material resources and recreation. Even such funda-mental assumptions as the belief in progress, in technology as a power for good and in man's ability to solve all his problems – all essential articles of secular faith not so very long ago – have now been shattered in many people's minds, while shared religious convictions and neatly self-contained systems of values are simi-larly being called into question. It would not be difficult to cite further examples of the contemporary crisis in accepted values, all of them indicative of a loss of wholeness, an increasing frag-mentation and specialization, a blurring of clarity and intelligibi-lity, an erosion of common ground – and what is essentially a process of denaturalization.

The grand design of mankind, nature and the animal kingdom, once bound together in a unified whole, is now felt to be threatened with disintegration. The relationship between humans and animals that particularly interests us here was the subject of a letter addres-sed to the President of the United States as long ago as 1855:

'What is mankind without animals?'

inquired the writer.

> 'If animals were to vanish from the face of the earth, mankind would perish in the solitude of his spirit. Whatever happens to animals, happens also to mankind. All things are interwoven; whatever touches the earth, touches mankind also.'

This vision of the *totality* of things is precisely what we have ceased to take for granted today – in the sciences and professions, no less than in our ordinary everyday relationships.

Whenever a self-evident mode of behaviour or set of beliefs and attitudes or some 'natural' unity ceases to be taken for granted, whenever feelings of uncertainty and vulnerability start to surface, then – and only then – do we begin to ask questions and mobilize the resources of scientific inquiry. Psychological research has tended to focus primarily on behaviour that is extraordinary, unintelligible, shocking or deviant. Hatred between members of different races, for example, has had a profound impact on the development of research into human prejudice. The notable failure of individuals to proffer assistance when faced with a road accident or an act of crime has prompted contemporary psychological research to examine the factors that inhibit or encourage helpful behaviour. The breakdown of sympathetic understanding between individuals, our inability to listen to other people, to discuss things with them in a spirit of tolerance and forgiveness, and the growing risk of social isolation and loneliness – all this has produced the paradoxical phenomenon of a mass-communication society in which communication difficulties and the factors that govern communication have become a central concern of contemporary scientific analysis, while the teaching of communication skills now occupies an important place in human behavioural training. In short, communication between individuals – and between humans and animals – is something we can no longer take for granted.

Likewise, a concern for animals in general and pets in particular has ceased to be an accepted part of life in a society that is becoming increasingly denaturalized – which is to say, among people who are now having to be re-educated into accepting that physical activity and physical training should be no less self-evident than a healthy diet, who did not automatically grow up in the company of animals – even if their childhood years were spent in the countryside (Kaufmann, 1976) – and whose encounters with the natural world and animals are often limited to what they see on film and television ('Lassie', 'Gentle Ben', etc.). The scientific study of the relationship between humans and animals, man and dog, is ultimately symptomatic of the dissolution of a symbiosis that was once taken for granted. This loss of wholeness has called into question the role of the dog in human development, giving rise to argument and controversy, to images of dog owners as 'friend' or 'foe', to questions about what a dog means to a person at different stages of his or her life, in different situations and personal circumstances, and what positive effects a dog may have on a person's life. Whether we like it or not, the relationship between man and animals is no longer taken for granted, while at the same time a wide-ranging environmental debate – for reasons that are not unconnected – has assumed outstanding topical importance. This explains why the relationship between man and animals has been 'rediscovered' in terms of its role in human development and upbringing and its contribution not only to the quality of human life, but also to mental health, general health care and therapy. Consequently, it has increasingly become a focus for systematic research. If initial studies concerned themselves with the role of animals in relation to specific clinical pictures and developmental disturbances, together with such specialized social situations as the isolation experienced by older people, this is because of the general tendency of psychological research to focus on phenomena that are extraordinary and *not* taken for granted – in a word, on the 'abnormal' (however one chooses to define that term). Of course, it is not unusual to discover, in the course of such research, that the line which separates the everyday from the exceptional is a remarkably fine one.

In the final analysis, therefore, scientific study of the relationship between man and animals is founded on uncertainty about phenomena and experiences that were formerly taken for granted – natural surroundings, social contacts, the regenerative powers of nature, and many other things that add up to 'quality of life'. As efforts are made to create a more humane environment, social observers are asking what part dogs might have to play in enhancing the quality of human life. This question may seem a little irrelevant, even exploitative: but history shows us countless examples of the happy co-existence of man and animals – a phenomenon that is copiously documented in the world's myths and religions, art and literature. Indeed, the prospect of man and animals co-existing in harmony has been described by Konrad Lorenz as something akin to 'a return to Paradise'.

The perspective from which we view people, material objects and animals undoubtedly influences our own perceptions, judgements and behaviour. Dogs, like any other phenomenon, can and should be viewed from a number of different perspectives. Only when we acknowledge that an object exists on many different levels – as part of the natural everyday scene, as the subject of artistic representation, as religious symbol and as material for scientific study and analysis – only then are we able to come to grips with the phenomenon in its complex totality, only then claim the right to an objective assessment.

2 The role of the dog in art and culture

Man's perception of himself, his place in the world, his social, cultural, religious and economic circumstances and constraints, are duly reflected in the significance he attaches to his animals. This means, of course, that the shared history of humans and animals has necessarily differed in kind at different historical epochs. Although that history has unfolded with a certain inevitability, everyday reality and images both positive and negative, together with their creative formulations and mythological roots, are all interdependent quantities subject to change. Hence the need to look briefly at the role of dogs in art and culture.

When man first began to live together with dogs, the latter undoubtedly acquired a universal importance in everyday human life. Dogs performed a number of useful physical functions, such as keeping watch over the house, the farmyards and the cattle, taking part in the hunt and serving as draught animals to pull sledges and carts. Furthermore, they fulfilled a variety of psychological needs as a playmate and companion for children and adults, sharing in their joys – and doubtless in their sorrows too.

The evolution of a society based on different estates or classes meant that the right to hunt became a privilege of the ruling class only. This led in turn to the creation of a kind of canine 'class system', in which the hunting hounds of the nobility were clearly set apart from the 'common' watchdogs owned by peasant farmers.

The Middle Ages witnessed the establishment of the first great hunting packs. One of the earliest writers on the subject of dogs was Baron Gaston de Foix (1331–1391), whose *Livre de Chasse* was published under the pseudonym Gaston Phoebus, and whose personal hunting pack is said to have numbered no less than 1600 hounds. During the Baroque period these large permanent packs ceased to be fashionable, although the hunt as such remained the lavish spectacle it had always been. During the hunting season the nobility simply made up the numbers by borrowing dogs from butchers and herdsmen – thereby saving themselves the considerable expense of feeding the dogs all the year round! But the right to maintain a hunting pack undoubtedly remained an exclusive prerogative of the ruling classes even in the post-Baroque era. Writing in 1828, Prince Hermann von Pückler-Muskau describes the hunting dogs kept by Earl of Harewood in England:

> 'What interested me most on this occasion, as being something entirely new to me, were the kennels for the hounds. There I discovered 150 hounds in two spotlessly clean chambers, each chamber provided with a large communal couch on which 75 dogs take their rest. Each of the chambers opens onto its own enclosed courtyard. No evil odours assailed the senses, nor was there any sign of uncleanliness. In each courtyard there is a standpipe with running water, and a servant is in attendance all day long, armed with a broom with which he sweeps the floor virtually without pause, sluicing it down with copious amounts of water. The dogs themselves are bred to the utmost obedience, and never soil their couch or the chamber. To feed them properly is a great art in itself, for in order to endure the great exertion of the chase they must be lean yet firm of flesh – like iron, each and every one.'

Early on in history dogs were also being bred for very different functions – to satisfy, as we might say today, a range of different emotional needs. These were dogs for women. In 1560 the Swiss naturalist Gesner, author of the *Historiae animalium*, received a letter from the Cambridge humanist John Caius listing the various breeds of English dog, in which he remarks:

> 'And we also have a small race of dogs that are specially bred to be the playthings of rich and noble ladies. The smaller they are, the more perfectly suited to their purpose, which is to be carried at the breast, in the bedchamber or in the lap, when their mistresses sally forth.'

The popularity of such dogs has continued undiminished down through the centuries, and few would doubt their beneficial impact on the quality of human life.

Alongside these so-called lapdogs – and not unconnected with the trends in fashionable society in the heyday of the French royal court – people began to breed certain types of dog for purely fashionable reasons. Poodles, for example, came into fashion at the time of Louis XVI. In the early decades of the nineteenth century pugs became popular in France, while in England the King Charles spaniel was superseded in fashionable circles by the Irish wolfhound. Collies were fashionable around the turn of the century, to be followed in the 1920s by Pekinese, fox terriers and Scotch terriers. Then came cocker spaniels, Alsatians, poodles once again, basset hounds and Yorkshire terriers. When systematic breeding was introduced at the start of the 20th century, there was a strong emphasis on breeding dogs with specific characteristics and skills to perform certain specialized functions (police dogs, search and rescue dogs, guide dogs for the blind, etc.).

The increasing individualization of human society is reflected in a more colourful and variegated canine world. As man's needs grow more complex, his environment changes to meet those needs – and dogs are a part of that environment. The desire for a dog, for an agreeable and sociable companion with which one can communicate, and which can also be taught to perform a range of useful functions, is undoubtedly rooted in a vital relationship between man and nature. But there are also other motives, meanings and functions which are partly rooted in the human personality and the specific environment of the individual. It should never be forgotten that the relationship between man and dog is a two-way process and can only be understood and explained as such.

The literature of dogs has a long history, beginning around 400 BC with Xenophon's *Kynegeticus*. It is important to note that for a thousand years the history of writings about dogs is essentially also a history of hunting. The first account of different breeds was written by John Caius, the Cambridge scholar referred to above. In his *De Canibus Britannicis* of 1570 he described the breeds indigenous to Britain at that time. In 1685 the first encyclopaedic study of dogs – *Cynographia Curiosa oder Hundebeschreibung* – appeared in Nuremberg from the pen of one Christian Franz Paullini. The book begins, as a matter of course, by cataloguing the various ways in which dogs enhance the quality of human life:

'The dog is the epitome of all Nature, and a storehouse of treasures. It is a refuge to the weary, an example to the true, a mirror of vigilance, an exemplar of understanding and constancy, a watchword and symbol to the wise – a creature justly famed in peace and war.'

The value placed on animals is always a reflection in part of the value placed on them by a particular society, culture or religion. Myths and religions serve to highlight the power and impotence of man and of animals alike. The conflict between good and evil extends beyond gods and humans to embrace animals as well, attesting once more to that natural unity of creation – man, nature and the animal kingdom – which was formerly taken for granted. Rules of conduct for associating with animals frequently derive from the cultural–religious standards and mores that map out the pattern of our relationships with other people, with animals and with the whole environment in which we live. This means that in many cases animals have not only a rational–functional meaning, but an emotional–mythological significance as well. In Greek mythology, for example, the wolf – the ancestor of all dogs – is a demonic creature, while the very same wolf becomes the creator of the world in the mythology of the North American Indians. In other words, the selfsame animal may be viewed in a totally different light by different cultures, which imbue it with a very different set of meanings.

The natural partnership between man and animals that was once taken for granted meant that dogs appear in literature at a very early stage. In Homer's *Odyssey* we read of 'Argus, Odysseus' long-suffering dog', who was the only one who recognized his master upon his return. The dog is a recurrent figure in the fables of Aesop (600 BC), Phaedrus (*c.*15 BC–*c.*AD 50), and Babrius (AD 200). We might also mention the dog Labes, who figures in Aristophanes' *The Wasps*. Stories about dogs occur throughout literature in many forms. In *A Midsummer Night's Dream* Shakespeare writes of dogs in these terms:

> 'My hounds are bred out of the Spartan kind,
> So flew'd, so sanded; and their heads are hung
> With ears that sweep away the morning dew;
> Crook-knee'd and dew-lapp'd like Thessalian bulls;
> Slow in pursuit, but match'd in mouth like bells,
> Each under each.'
> *Act IV, Scene I*

Moving on to the 19th century we meet Aso, the dog owned by the Jew Abdias in Adalbert Stifter's *Studien*, while Marie von Ebner-Eschenbach writes about the exotically-named 'Krambambuli'. The bull terrier 'Garm' is just one of many canine stalwarts who feature in the work of Rudyard Kipling. We could also mention 'Berganza', the eponymous hero of E.T.A. Hoffmann's *Nachricht von den neuesten Schicksalen des Hundes Berganza* [News of the Most Recent Fortunes of the Dog Berganza]; the boxer 'Nick' in the exchange of letters *From Dog to Dog* by R. Katz; the little dog 'Mumu' in Nikolai Gogol's tales of the same name; the dachshund 'Schnipp Fidelius Adelzahn' in the novel of that name by Sven Fleuron; or *Das Scheusal* [The Monster] by Alice Herdan-Zuckmayer.

Dogs in literature often have their counterparts in real life, so it is not surprising that the influence of dogs on the quality of human life should have found its most forceful, vivid and positive expression in literature, long before this subject came under the scrutiny of analytical–empirical science. It will be helpful, therefore, to examine one or two further instances of the literary treatment of the classic 'dog and master' relationship. Literature and art can contribute significantly to the formulation of plausible investigative hypotheses. The fact that this contribution has been largely ignored by experimental psychologists is primarily due to the one-sidedness of their approach in many instances and their frequent refusal to depart from chosen research models.

In his novella *Herr und Hund*, Thomas Mann describes what life is like in the company of the mongrel gun dog Bauschan:

'His life consists in waiting to go out for his next walk, and the waiting begins as soon as he has fully recovered from his last outing. Even at night he is waiting, for his periods of sleep are distributed throughout the entire 24-hour daily cycle.'

Literature also contains striking instances of the idea that dogs can embody certain positive human characteristics, that they may exhibit qualities which are conspicuously absent in many of one's fellow men. Arthur Schopenhauer, whom no-one could possibly accuse of excessive philanthropy, also reflects on the 'intelligence of animals' and concludes that it would have been better for man to be descended from dogs instead of apes, since the former are the only creatures endowed with a form of self-expression akin to human laughter, namely tail-wagging:

'How favourably this form of greeting instilled in him by nature compares with the obsequious bows and polite grunts of humans, whose protestations of sincere friendship and devotion are a thousand times less to be believed – at least for the present time.

Dogs are rightly regarded as the epitome of loyalty . . . Where else shall one find refuge from the endless dissimulation, falsehood and treachery of humans, if not in dogs, upon whose honest countenance one can gaze without mistrust.'

We might also mention Elisabeth Russell, who contrasts human inconstancy with the unfailing affection of dogs, thus invoking one of the most valued experiences in human life:

'I would like to begin by pointing out that parents, husbands, children, lovers and friends are all very well in their way: but they are not dogs. In the course of my life I have been all of these things in turn – except that I was a wife instead of a husband – so I know what I am talking about. I know all about the ups and downs, the daily, not to say hourly, changes in mood that seem to be a necessary concomitant of love for us over-sensitive humans. Dogs are not subject to these shifts in mood. When they give their love, they give it for good, true to their dying breath. That is how I should like to be loved – and that is why I want to talk about dogs.'

The list of literary references to the special quality of the relationship between man and dog is by no means exhausted. We might recall Christian Fürchtegott Gellert's fable *Die beiden Hunde* [The Two Dogs], Christian Morgenstern's 'Heroic Poodle' –and the humorous poem by Heinrich Heine entitled *The Virtuous Dog*. It is worth pointing out, however, that not everyone who has written on the subject of dogs is necessarily a dog-lover. Goethe resigned as Director of the Weimar Theatre because the comedian Karsten had been allowed to put on the play *Der Hund des Aubry* with his famous performing poodle. Goethe expressed himself in these terms to Schiller:

'The theatre stage is not a kennel or a home for curs.
Enter poodle, exit poet: no artist to a dog defers.'

It is perhaps indicative of Goethe's general feelings about dogs that Mephistopheles chooses to enter Faust's life in the guise of a black poodle. Otherwise dogs do *not* appear to have been a favourite subject of his writing: if he mentions them at all, it is only to complain about the fearful noise they make with their 'incessant yapping and barking'.

To use the language of economics, it could be said that the costs and benefits of dog ownership are apparent in literature as they are in life, but that the positive aspects – in terms of a dog's stabilizing influence on human behaviour and its contribution to the quality of human life – outweigh the negative. This corresponds closely to the findings of empirical research – as we shall see below.

Painting and sculpture provide further clues to the importance that man has attached – and continues to attach – to animals and dogs in particular. Every known breed of dog must have been reproduced pictorially in one form or another. The earliest representations of animals were cave paintings, whose very existence attests to the central role of animals in human development. Dogs have been a recurrent motif throughout the history of art: the 'molossians' or mastiffs of the ancients and the diminutive lapdogs of the Rococo, the hunting dogs of the Baroque and the English 19th century, the dogs of light and shade painted by the Impressionists, the stylized greyhounds of art nouveau, and the work of the photo-realists, who painted their dogs virtually hair by hair.

Our images of Queen Elizabeth II would hardly be complete without the dogs – corgis – which appear in her portraits. These pictures continue the great tradition of Titian, who portrayed the Emperor Charles V with a mastiff, as a symbol of power, and Velazquez, who invariably painted the Spanish Habsburgs surrounded by their dogs. In all these works the dogs are standing, sitting or lying next to their masters in the role of bodyguards, valiant companions in the chase, symbols of power, vitality and loyal devotion.

Dogs serve as symbolic figures in many paintings. In Van Eyck's *The Marriage of Giovanni Arnolfini and Giovanna Cenani* the little Maltese dog in the foreground symbolizes fidelity. In all the banquet scenes painted by Paolo Veronese, dogs are portrayed with extreme realism as man's natural companions – as indeed they are in earlier works by painters of the Middle Ages.

In 1752 Tiepolo painted the ceiling of the episcopal Residenz in Würzburg, depicting the induction of Bishop Arnulf by the Emperor Frederick: and in the centre of the scene is a dog. Bellini's *View of a Palazzo* portrays dogs and horses as an integral part of daily life. But dogs were not always confined to an incidental role in paintings. Sometimes they were the actual subjects of portraits. The whole sub-genre of 'dog portraits' was created by Piero di Cosimo with *The Death of Procris*, in which the mourning dog appears to enjoy equality of status with the humans. In 1521 Albrecht Dürer included a drawing of a *Recumbent Dog* in the sketchbook of his Netherlands journey, and a drawing for the portrait of a dog by Jacopo Bassano has survived from the year 1575. At the end of the 16th century Goltzius produced a life-size portrait of his dog. Gainsborough portrayed a Pomeranian together with its litter. Jean Baptiste Audrey, Louis XV's court painter, began by painting the King's dogs, then went on to produce many portraits of dogs to special commission. The fashion for such portraits was continued among the English aristocracy of the 19th century, with their passionate fondness for hunting. George Stubbs, Jacques-Laurent Gasse, Benjamin Marshall and Sir Edwin Landseer all painted many portraits both of horses and of dogs.

If dogs in art and literature are seen to reflect and interpret the relationship between humans and animals, it is only proper that this brief and necessarily incomplete survey should spare a passing glance for pictorial narratives and even comic strips, in which dogs appear as companions to humans, or indeed as the principal character. Those that come to mind include 'Plisch und Plum', created by Wilhelm Busch, Obelix and his constant companion, the tiny 'Idefix', or the fox terrier 'Snowy', Tin-Tin's helpmate in the Herge comic strip. And what child – or indeed adult – is not familiar with Walt Disney's Pluto or Snoopy from *Peanuts,* that affectionate caricature and modern archetype of the dog with human attributes? In this way dogs have become a part of the mass communications industry, which in turn serves as a bridge between humans and dogs.

Whether dogs might be a suitable subject for musical treatment, following the huge success of *Cats*, is something on which we can only speculate. But there can be no doubt that dogs are now an integral part of our cultural environment, thanks to the efforts of those writers, poets and painters who have chosen dogs as the subject of their works. When dogs also become a focus of scientific attention, not only in veterinary medicine and behavioural research, but also in empirical social science, psychology and therapeutics, these literary and artistic interpretations furnish a valuable basis for scientific inquiry.

3   Dogs and personality

The relationship between man and dog is now coming under scrutiny from many different perspectives. This renewed interest is also reflected in the growing number of scientific studies dealing with the quality, intensity, significance and consequences of the man–dog relationship.

Any empirical investigation of the interrelationships between dogs, humans and the quality of life must begin with a critical review of the extant scientific literature. This is essential in order to develop a theoretical model that can serve as a point of departure for further investigations.

The review of that literature undertaken in the following pages aims at summarizing the present state of scientific knowledge in this field. A study was made of all the relevant titles published between 1965 and 1983 which appear in *Psychological Abstracts,* *'Dimdi'* and the catalogue of the Zentralstelle für psychologische Information und Dokumentation. The material included both empirical and theoretical studies, as well as studies concerned with the question of plausibility. Some difficulties were experienced in obtaining literature of a semi-private nature (congress reports and research reports for internal circulation abroad), as well as certain less accessible foreign journals and dissertations. Selected publications dealing with the problems of pet ownership in general were also consulted, in so far as they contained specific information relating to the topic under consideration.

It should be emphasized at the outset that none of the studies examined attempts to establish a coherent theoretical framework. They consist for the most part of surveys of the advantages and disadvantages of dog ownership, personality studies of dog owners based on psychological tests, studies on the role of dogs in therapy, as aids to child rearing, and as companions for the elderly and the blind – together with various discussions dealing with questions of plausibility. Interestingly enough, there appears to be virtually nothing on this subject published in German. But this in turn is merely symptomatic of the more general neglect noted by Mugford (1980, p. 119):

15

'After studying the available literature on the relationship between animals and humans, one can only concur with Levinson (1974) when he concludes that this area remains the *terra incognita,* so to speak, of modern psychology.'

A study of the available scientific literature revealed essentially six distinct areas of interest:

1. The personality traits of dog owners, with particular reference to the ways in which attitudes to dogs are influenced by attitudes to humans and vice versa.
2. The therapeutic use of dogs in the treatment of physical and mental illness, and their role in relation to the blind, prison inmates and other social subgroups.
3. The role of dogs in the development of children, adults and senior citizens.
4. Dogs and dog owners as a topic for public debate and a target for prejudice.
5. Dogs and public health: aspects of dog ownership relating to hygiene.
6. Observations and reports on the cost–benefit aspects of dog ownership – from a practical and psychological point of view.

At the same time dogs are clearly an important focus of attention in behavioural research, i.e. the scientific study of animal behaviour together with its changes and motivation. Any detailed consideration of these findings – which also deal with such matters as the social behaviour of dogs, their 'language' and their ability to communicate – would exceed the scope of the present study. But our understanding of the interaction between humans and dogs will be usefully enhanced by an extended quotation from a recent paper by the behaviouralist Dorit Feddersen-Petersen:

'Dogs see us as part of their world, and they participate in our lives. In a word, they are our partners and the relationship between dogs and humans is a two-way process. This particular form of cohabitation is by no means without its problems. The primary reason for this is that dogs view us as fellow members of the canine species and they treat us more or less consistently as such. They "caninize" us, so to speak. The same tendency to assimilate occurs in humans, who are only too ready to interpret the behaviour of dogs in human terms. The temptation to anthropomorphize animal behaviour is deeply rooted within us and we succumb very easily.

This can lead to serious misunderstandings, mishaps – even acts of cruelty to the animals concerned. Dogs are not human beings in a different guise, but highly developed social mammals with a strong sense of hierarchy.

Their speech is largely directed towards the particular individual who is their daily companion. It is to this person that they communicate their intentions, and to whose actions and reactions they attend. We should make an effort to understand this speech and acquaint ourselves with the biological foundations of canine behaviour . . . All house dogs are basically alike in their social behaviour, their highly developed powers of communication and their attachment to gregarious forms of living. In order to understand the biological roots of canine behaviour we need to know something about their ancestors who lived in the wild . . . All house dogs are descended from wolves.'
(Dorit Feddersen-Petersen, 1984)

Reflections such as these on the interaction between humans and dogs give rise to a whole series of questions which have tended to be ignored even by behaviouralists. What purpose or purposes do dogs serve in human society? And what is the possible impact on a dog of different kinds of human social behaviour? The answers to these questions should enable us to arrive at a considered view of what a person should or should not do in the dog's own best interests. If the relationship between man and dog really *is* one of mutual dependency, then this aspect of the relationship cannot be ignored. Humans are often cruel to animals in the name of science by performing painful – and sometimes unnecessary – experiments on them. But they may also tyrannize animals and make them neurotic without deliberate scientific intent. In its way such behaviour is also a form of 'experimentation'. It attracts no public protest, but is no less common and ultimately no less cruel. In this connection it is interesting to note the publication of studies by Tortora (1978) on the problems and methods of behavioural therapy with animals, and Borcheld (1983) on potential behavioural problems in dogs caused by cohabitation with humans. Even under 'normal' conditions, however, it has been shown that there is a clear correlation between the way dogs are treated by humans and the way they (the dogs) subsequently behave (see *inter alia* Rubin and Beck, 1982).

Having studied the available scientific literature on the relationship between man and dog, we shall now proceed to a systematic discussion of our findings.

Man and dog: the personality of dog owners

The principal credit for elevating the relationship between man and dog to the status of a subject for serious psychological inquiry belongs to Levinson (see Levinson, 1962; 1964; 1965; 1969; 1970; 1972; 1975; 1978; 1980; 1982). He rightly stresses that there are two possible approaches to the subject, which excites both positive and negative feelings in people:

1. the 'intuitive' (or as we might also call it, the 'naive') approach, which assumes 'a continuum between the animal kingdom and man' (Levinson, 1982, p. 284) that ultimately determines – and explains – the quality of the resulting relationship between man and animal; and
2. the scientific approach, which is primarily concerned to organize its subject matter in a logical manner and conduct systematic research into specific aspects.

Levinson's work led him to define the following major areas of research:

- Animals and human personality development;
- Communication between man and animals and the consequences thereof;
- Animals as companions and 'co-therapists'.

These various aspects will be considered in more detail later. To begin with, we shall look at studies that attempt to describe and explain the psychological relationship between human personality and dogs. Some of these examine the self-image of dog owners, others look at the characteristics they attribute to their dogs. Another group of studies focusses on the quality of interpersonal relations, and the effect this has on the relationship with an animal. Finally, a third group of studies proceeds on the assumption that dog ownership can be described and explained in terms of specific personality traits, as measured by standard psychological tests.

Dog owners: self-image and attitudes to one's own dog

It is often said that a dog owner resembles his dog in certain ways, even down to his physical appearance. We all know that people can be very fanciful – not to mention dogmatic – about detecting physical resemblances between a baby and one or other of its parents or grandparents. The idea that humans and animals may exhibit certain facial similarities led Aristotle (384–322 BC) to speak of a person having, for example, 'the face of a donkey' and to infer from this that a person with such a face is also 'like a donkey' in character. All 'physiognomists' (to give them their correct historical name) believe in a direct correlation and interaction between body and soul, between specific identifiable forms of the body and head and specific psychological traits. However, our research failed to uncover any studies dealing with physiognomic or constitutional resemblances between humans and dogs, not even at the level of opinion or prejudice.

One of the first important points to note is that the behaviour of a dog, like that of any animal, is not simply 'described', but characterized with reference to specific psychological features and attributes in much the same way as human behaviour. In a word, the dog is anthropomorphized – which means, more often than not, that characteristics which are socially desirable in a human being are readily projected onto a dog. In a small study conducted some years ago we asked a group of 60 dog owners to describe their own dogs (Bergler, 1964). Their answers are summarized and reprinted in descending order of frequency in Table 1 below: taken together, they form a comprehensive psychogram of dogs as perceived by their owners.

Table 1 Characteristics of a dog as perceived by dog owners (spontaneous replies)

loyal, devoted, absolute loyalty, knows where he belongs, wants to be where his master is, wouldn't go off with anyone else

quick to learn, clever, bright, very sharp, intelligent

would lay down his life for his master, knows and accepts that he belongs to his master, is completely at his master's beck and call, accepts authority

understands people, intelligent, only dogs have a genuinely close relationship with humans, dogs can tell who likes them and who doesn't

docile, obedient, adaptable, does what his master wants, disciplined

Table 1 *contd*

so pleased when you come home, shows more pleasure than any other kind of pet, very demonstrative

feels responsible for us, wants to guard and protect us, I always feel safe with the dog

they have a better disposition than lots of humans, are often more loyal than humans, a dog never lets you down, never has any ulterior motive, the more I see of people, the more I like animals, dogs are the most loyal creatures on God's earth

they are always grateful, they don't cause people any trouble, don't ever want to be a nuisance or a burden

they like to show affection, always friendly, like to play, likes to fool about

touchy, easily offended, can be mortally offended, very sensitive, jealous because he has to share love with others, wouldn't let anybody near our child

often understands you better than other people, dogs are often a lot more sensitive about humans, often cleverer than human beings

it's not hard for people to understand dogs and see what it is they want

sees us as belonging to the pack, wants to share with a human being as the head of the pack, likes to have everyone gathered together

---

There is no doubt that people are prepared to regard dogs as absolutely loyal and trustworthy partners. Dogs possess certain attributes that are seen to be socially desirable in humans, but whose presence in the human character is apparently not something that can be taken for granted. This image of one's own dog, as projected by dog owners, may now be compared with the owners' self-image. Referring back once more to the above-mentioned pilot study – and without claiming that the results are wholly representative – we find that the characteristics associated with a 'typical' dog owner by dog owners themselves may be tabulated as follows (again, in descending order of frequency):

Table 2   Characteristics of a typical dog owner (spontaneous replies)

---

animal-loving, must be sympathetic to animals, must be fond of animals, sticks up for animals

easy-going, tolerant, affable, placid, well-balanced, even-tempered, is also patient with people

Table 2 *contd*

sensitive, understanding, kind, warm-hearted, more feeling

good-natured, helpful, pleasant, friendly

likes other people, gets on well with people, anyone who likes animals also likes people – particularly young children

nature-loving, is more interested in nature, likes to be outdoors, is fond of walking, is more the outdoor type

doesn't like to be alone, is gregarious

not so set in his ways, open-minded, receptive, natural, not uptight, frank, easy-going, more free and easy

not so pernickety, not fussy, can't afford to be excessively house-proud

maternal, caring

people who need love and sympathy

must be willing to make sacrifices, not self-centred, not mean, not petty-minded, not tight with their money

---

In other words, dog owners associate socially desirable characteristics not only with their dogs, but also with themselves. For them, the principal characteristics of the typical dog owner are a love of animals, an easy-going nature, tolerance, sensitivity and depth of feeling. Dog owners see themselves as good-natured, helpful people, who like their fellow men as much as they like animals, and are generally gregarious, open-minded and nature-loving.

These findings raise a number of fundamental questions. Is the way a person describes his dog directly related to the way that person sees himself – or would like to see himself, perhaps (i.e. an ideal self-image)? Is the dog a creature whose 'character' is a mirror image of our own attributes and traits – or fantasies? Could it be that we project our own hopes and desires, our fears and shortcomings onto our dogs? Alternatively, does a dog possess certain characteristics that we perceive as supplementing or complementing our own behavioural repertoire?

It is extremely difficult to find any empirical studies offering direct answers to these questions – although it is possible to put forward a variety of interesting theories based on research into interpersonal attraction (Bergler, 1982) and the factors that have been found to influence such attraction (physical attractiveness, similarities in outlook, etc.). One study by Quinn-Kevins (1983) takes as its starting point the hypothesis that when owners of dogs and cats describe their pets they invariably furnish information about themselves in the process – in other words, that characterizations of pets are also essentially characterizations of self. The questionnaire used in the study included a scale of personality characteristics, and respondents were invited to describe both their dogs and their own personalities in terms of these characteristics. Their answers confirmed the initial premise of the study: when people describe their dogs, they also tell us a good deal about themselves. The 'status' of the dog – whether mongrel or thoroughbred – had no influence on this pattern of self-revelation.

If there really *is* a correlation between the way people describe their dogs and the way they describe their own personalities, and if this is an important factor in determining perceptions of the relationship betweeen dog and master, then this in turn raises a further (and more fundamental) question – namely, to what extent the quality of this relationship may affect the behaviour of dog owners vis-à-vis their fellow human beings.

Dog owners: their attitudes to dogs and to their fellow human beings

A number of studies have taken as their starting point the question of whether there exists a correlation between the attitudes of pet owners to people and their attitudes to their pets. More specifically, does a positive relationship between master and dog enable us to make a reliable prediction about that person's behaviour towards other people? Or to put the question the other way round: are a person's difficulties in relating to his fellow human beings sometimes reflected in the way he treats his dog?

The number of studies on this subject is too small to furnish any definitive answers, and the published findings are to some extent contradictory – partly, no doubt, because individual studies differ so widely in their theory and method.

Brown, Shaw and Kirkland (1972) investigated the hypothesis that affection for other people is a function of affection for dogs. A sample of 200 students was divided into two groups on the basis of self-assessment on a scale from 'I hate dogs' to 'I am crazy about dogs'. Affection for other people was measured using the six scales devised by Schultz (1958) for his 'Fundamental Interpersonal Relations Orientation Behavior Test' (FIRO). The authors found that people who have little affection for, or interest in, dogs are generally not very affectionate or attentive towards other people either. However, this did not apply to the extreme group of so-called 'dog freaks', whose interest in their fellow human beings was shown to be relatively limited. In other words, these findings tend to support the view that the specific quality of a person's emotional attachment to a dog partly determines the specific quality of his or her feelings for other people as well – with the proviso that an *extreme* love for dogs is seen to be detrimental to interpersonal attachments. The findings of Brown *et al.* (1972) were subsequently confirmed by Lee in his study of 1976.

The study by Cameron *et al.* (1966) adopts a different approach. Instead of looking at individual degrees of attachment to dogs and cats, the authors studied pet owners and non pet owners on the basis of questions such as 'How much do other people like you?' and 'How much do you like other people?' They were then asked to select the appropriate answers on a 16-point scale ranging from 'very much' to 'not at all'. Although the findings did not reveal any significant differences between pet owners and non pet owners, the authors nevertheless speak of a tendency for pet owners to like people *less,* generally speaking, than non pet owners. In a follow-up study by Cameron and Mattson (1972) it was found that non pet owners like people significantly more than they like animals, whereas pet owners prefer their pets to other people (although even this difference is only significant at the 7% level). Using the scale devised by Eysenck ('Neuroticism and Extraversion': see Eysenck and Eysenck, 1969), the authors found no differences between pet owners and non pet owners. One further finding is of interest here. Urban pet owners as a group scored lower than other subjects on Canter's 'Ego Strength' scale (a shorter version of Barron's Ego Strength scale). 'Ego strength' refers here to a person's ability to order, regulate and control his emotional needs. Cameron and Mattson (1972) concluded from these scores that pet owners living in an urban environment have a lower level of mental health than non pet owners. What exactly they mean by this, however, and the manner in which they arrive at such a conclusion, are not at all clear. At all events, their findings are not backed up by solid empirical evidence.

The nature of a person's attitude to animals, and the effect this has on attitudes to other people, must also be viewed in relation to the different types of pet (dog, cat, etc.). In a study of dog owners and cat owners conducted by Kidd and Kidd (1980), the subjects were asked how much they like adults and children. No differences were found between the sexes, but there was a very clear difference with regard to preferred pet type. Cat lovers were found to like children and adults significantly less than dog lovers did. While these findings clearly show that personality differences were also related to preferred pet type, there is insufficient data to establish the existence of a direct causal link – i.e. to tell us how far the chosen pet influences the owner's personality, or, conversely, how far the choice of a particular pet type is determined by the owner's personality.

Hitherto we have proceeded on the assumption that the nature of a person's attitude to a dog tells us something about his general attitude to his fellow human beings. However, given the strong tendency of humans to anthropomorphize dogs, we should also be asking the question the other way round, so to speak – i.e. can a person's experiences of other people, either as a child or in the course of his adult development, have a specific influence on attitudes and behaviour towards animals in general and dogs in particular? Research has in fact shown that the sequence of cause and effect can work in this direction too.

Sherick (1981) describes a three-year course of psychotherapy with a young girl who was six years old when she embarked on the course. The girl had a pet dog, wanted a rabbit as well, and was very fond of animals in general. She also wanted to become a vet. According to Sherick, the way in which the girl treated her dog was a direct reflection of the way the child had always been treated by her parents. The pet helped her to express the feelings she had for her mother, her father and her elder brother. The therapist describes how the girl adopted a model 'parental' role towards her dog, reflecting her own experience of the parent-child relationship. On the one hand she was very practical and efficient, devoting a great deal of her time to looking after the dog. On the other hand, according to Sherick, the relationship was also coloured by strong aggressive and libidinous desires. The intense longing for a rabbit – in Sherick's psychoanalytical interpretation – is a symbolic expression of the emptiness and parental rejection experienced on occasions by the patient. The desire to own a horse, subsequently expressed by the girl during therapy, is interpreted as a form of penis envy. Independently of the attempt to elucidate a particular relationship between a human and an animal in terms of a specific pattern of parental upbringing, and to explain this through psychoanalysis, the author also underlines the very important role that animals can play in therapy with children – and touches on the possibility of their use in adult therapy as well.

The correlation between the treatment of children by their parents and the treatment of animals is also examined in another study by De Viney, Dickert and Lockwood (1983). In the context of a family therapy programme questions were put to members of

200 families where child abuse had occurred in one form or another (physical or sexual abuse, total neglect of the home). In particular, the authors wanted to find out to what extent the animals in pet-owning families within the sample were also subjected to mal-treatment – and whether this occurred primarily at the hands of a child-abusing parent. Pet abuse was defined as failure to care for the animal in a proper fashion, or conduct leading to the death of the animal, whether through physical violence (beating) or neg-lect. As an important preliminary finding the authors cited the fact that in the 19 families where physical abuse of children had been definitely established, abuse of animals had also occurred. No cor-relation was found between other forms of child abuse and the mal-treatment of pets. The authors concede that they are not yet in a position to comment on any more specific correlations which may exist between particular forms of child abuse and particular forms of pet abuse.

The opposite approach is adopted in a study by Schmitt and Kempe (1975; cited after Kidd and Kidd, 1980), which found that parents were less likely to abuse their children if they themselves had grown up with pets in the parental home. Kidd and Kidd infer from this (1980, p. 947) that the absence of a pet in the parental home may increase aggressiveness towards children. Aggressive-ness, they point out, is the only personality trait where the subjects' scores deviate from the normal values for adults given by Edwards; other traits, such as dominance and helpfulness, show no such deviation.

We come finally to a study by Rynearson (1978), which consists of three case studies (all women). Again, the author starts from specific forms of disturbed interpersonal relations and proceeds to investigate their impact on relationships between humans and animals. The subjects were found to be excessively protective towards animals and anxiously attached to them – behaviour which is attributed to the absence in their early lives of the kind of refer-ence person who is so vital for the development of healthy interper-sonal relations later on. According to Rynearson, this motivational state forms the basis for a total identification with the animal: in all three reported cases the animal represents that part of the woman's personality which she was never able to show in her relations with other people.

The evidence clearly shows that a relationship of mutual depen-dency exists between humans and animals. Interpersonal behaviour and attitudes are therefore bound to influence the way we relate to a dog (for example), which in turn influences the animal's own behaviour. To that extent, animal behaviour is always in part a reflection of human behaviour. It is evidently possible to project both positive and negative experiences with other human beings onto a dog. Equally, the animal may be seen as the fulfilment of certain desires and longings, often of an unconscious nature – something that is particularly likely to occur in situations where other people are unable (or unwilling) to satisfy such needs.

Clearly this is not a matter of simple cause and effect, and further research is needed to illuminate the complex mechanisms at work here. One very important factor is the role dogs play in an individual's personal development. Childhood experiences with pets have a decisive and lasting influence on later adult attitudes towards animals. This kind of correlation has been demonstrated by Serpell (1981), who took as his point of departure the 1980 study by Kidd and Kidd, in which it was shown that people who have grown up with a particular type of pet in their childhood and youth – such as a dog – retain a strong affection for this type of pet in later life.

All the studies discussed so far have centred on the idea that humans and animals are engaged in a process of interaction. We now turn to a group of studies which adopt a rather different approach, based on theories of personality. Ownership or non-ownership of a dog or other pets is explained with reference to specific personality traits, while behaviour is explained variously in terms of genetic factors and acquired or learned dispositions.

Dog owners: personality and dog ownership

An explanation of human behaviour is only possible if we recognize that the latter is a result of the individual's interaction with the specific set of cultural, economic and social conditions that circumscribe his or her life. Although this is hardly a novel insight, deriving as it does from Lewin's 'field theory', there still exists a school of thought in differential psychology today which is essentially rooted in simplistic popular psychology. I refer to the idea that human development leads first to the formation of specific personality traits, which are then supposed to 'explain' human behaviour. All kinds of so-called personality tests have been devised on the basis of this assumption, and there is virtually no subject of psychological research, no observable form of behaviour, which has not been explained with reference to 'personality factors' of one sort or another. Neither widespread scientific criticism of these tests nor the inadequate explanation and prediction value of such methods have succeeded in undermining their popularity in the eyes of psychologists and laymen alike. This ostensibly scientific approach to personality is in fact little more than crude popular psychology masquerading under another name. But since this approach has had a significant influence on past research into pet ownership, our review of the literature would not be complete without a discussion of these studies, notwithstanding our serious reservations about their methodological soundness. The question that must always be asked is this: to what extent can a specific form of behaviour be explained in terms of specific personality traits? In fact, this question is hardly ever posed, let alone considered fully in terms of its many implications.

Demographic characteristics of dog owners

Demographic data on dog and pet owners (age, income, social status, level of education, etc.) are given in two national surveys of pet ownership carried out by Goodwin in Great Britain (1975) and the MAFO Institute in West Germany (1984).

Goodwin's study shows that 49% of households in Great Britain own a pet of some kind, while 51% of this group are dog owners. In other words, 25% of all the households in Britain own one or more dogs. Social status was not found to be a significant factor in pet ownership. One finding that stands out particularly is that the highest percentage of pets occurs in families with children between the ages of 6 and 15. It is also interesting to note that the percentage of households with pets increases with the size of the household. Fifty-five per cent of dog owners say that they keep their dogs as pets, i.e. not for exclusively practical reasons such as personal security, hunting, etc.

When we examine the reasons for dog ownership, we find that socio-economic status is indeed a significant factor. Seventy-three per cent of upper-class and upper middle-class households own a dog purely as a pet, while the corresponding figure for low-income families is only 44% (Goodwin, 1975).

Tabulated below (Table 3) are the demographic characteristics of dog owners, owners of other pets and non pet owners, as revealed by a representative survey of the West German population (i.e. not just a random sample of households) carried out by the MAFO Institute in 1984, based on a total sample of 4000 people:

Table 3   Demographic characteristics

	Total	Respondents with dog in household	Respondents with other pets in household	Respondents with no pets in household
	n = 4038 (100)	n = 625 (15.5)	n = 954 (23.6)	n = 2459 (60.9)
		(%)		
Age				
14–19 years	12	14	16	10
20–29 years	16	17	18	16
30–39 years	14	17	15	13
40–49 years	18	20	23	15
50–59 years	15	16	14	15
60–69 years	12	9	9	13
70 years and older	13	8	6	17
Educational qualifications or last school attended				
Primary and trade school, no certificate	25	23	20	27
Primary and trade school w. certificate	44	39	46	44
Secondary school, no school-leaving exam./ several yrs. at business or technical college	23	30	25	21
School-leaving exam.	4	4	4	4
College/university	3	4	3	3
None stated	1	1	1	1
Family status				
Single	23	25	28	21
Married	62	66	62	60
Widowed/divorced/ separated	14	8	10	18
None stated	1	–	1	1
Occupational status				
Working full time	48	52	53	44
Not working	52	48	47	56

Table 3 *contd*

	Total	Respondents with dog in household	Respondents with other pets in household	Respondents with no pets in household
	n = 4038 (100)	n = 625 (15.5)	n = 954 (23.6) (%)	n = 2459 (60.9)

Type of work

Owners or managers of large companies, company directors	–	1	–	–
Self-employed businessmen, owners of small firms, self-employed skilled tradesmen	4	6	2	4
Liberal professions	1	1	1	1
Senior clerical grades	3	3	3	3
Other clerical grades	30	30	33	29
Senior officials	1	1	1	1
Officials, other grades	4	5	3	3
Skilled workers, skilled tradesmen employed by others	20	17	21	20
Other wage earners	15	11	13	17
Self-employed farmers	2	3	2	1
Agricultural labourers	1	1	–	1
Other/never in work	10	10	10	11
None stated	9	10	11	9

Combined household income*

Less than DM 999	4	3	3	5
DM 1000–1499	10	7	7	12
DM 1500–1999	16	12	14	18
DM 2000–2499	18	17	17	18
DM 2500–2999	15	17	18	13
DM 3000–3499	12	11	17	10
DM 3500 or more	16	25	17	13
None stated	9	7	8	10

Table 3 *contd*

	Total	Respondents with dog in household	Respondents with other pets in household	Respondents with no pets in household
	n = 4038 (100)	n = 625 (15.5)	n = 954 (23.6)	n = 2459 (60.9)
		(%)		
No. of people in household				
1 person	14	5	8	19
2 persons	30	22	22	36
3 persons	23	25	27	21
4 persons	21	29	28	16
5 persons or more	12	18	5	9
No. of children and adolescents in household				
Children below the age of 6	10	12	11	9
Children aged between 6 and 14	18	23	25	14
Adolescents aged between 14 and 18	24	34	33	19
Social status (interviewer's assessment)				
Upper class	2	6	2	1
Upper middle class	25	32	28	23
Lower middle class	62	54	60	64
Working class	11	9	10	12
Sex				
Male	46	46	49	45
Female	54	54	51	55
Size of locality (no. of residents)				
up to 1999	7	11	6	6
2000–4999	10	11	12	9
5000–19 999	23	28	25	21
20 000–99 999	27	30	27	26
100 000–499 999	15	11	15	17
500 000 or more	18	10	15	20

*The amounts have been expressed in DM as in the original survey.
At the time of English publication, the exchange rate was 3.03 DM = £1.00.

The general picture of dog owners that emerges from this survey may be summarized as follows:

- They are somewhat younger than the average
- Their level of education is somewhat above the average
- They are at the higher end of the income scale
- They belong with above-average frequency to the upper middle class and upper class
- They live with above-average frequency in larger households with children and adolescents

As far as occupational status and type of work are concerned, there are no significant differences between the various groups. All in all, demographic characteristics of this kind are of minimal value in terms of 'explaining' the ownership of dogs or other pets (Bergler, 1982). One point of interest does emerge, however. Notwithstanding the large number of research findings which indicate that a dog has a very positive psychological value for single persons living alone, particularly the elderly, pet ownership is far more widespread among families with children than among the elderly and unattached.

Personality characteristics of dog owners

As was stated earlier, dog owners and non-owners have been characterized and categorized in terms of every imaginable personality trait, utilizing a wide range of test procedures and diagnostic methods. The instruments used include both general personality tests and attitudinal scales, which provide a vehicle for self-description and self-report by asking subjects to respond to a list of statements designed to reveal various aspects of human personality.

At a popular level of debate pet ownership is often 'explained' in terms of a general love of animals, which is cited as the central 'motive' for this behaviour. This approach is typical of a certain school of psychology which always associates a specific, observable form of human behaviour – such as dog ownership – with a specific drive or capacity; in this case, a 'love of animals'. The drive gives rise to the behaviour (it is supposed) by a simple process of cause and effect. But love of animals does not appear to be reason enough in itself for buying a dog. After all, many people who claim to love animals do not own a dog. However, there does appear to be a correlation between the *degree* of self-reported love for animals and the *number* of pets kept. In a study of 223 pet owners,

Kidd and Kidd (1980) found that persons who describe themselves as 'dog lovers' keep an average of two dogs, but hardly ever a cat, while persons who describe themselves as 'cat lovers' keep an average of two cats – and very rarely a dog. It turned out that dog lovers had owned significantly fewer cats in their childhood and cat lovers significantly fewer dogs – which points to the strong influence of the parental home on pet preferences.

Love of animals alone, therefore, does not suffice to explain ownership or non-ownership of a pet. Nor is it possible to predict with any certainty what type of pet a self-avowed animal lover will acquire.

It is not surprising, therefore, that Kidd, Kelly and Kidd (1983) should have chosen to study the question of how far owners of different pet types can be clearly distinguished in terms of personality characteristics. Two hundred owners of horses, snakes, pigeons and caged birds were approached by letter – through vets, pet shops and pet clubs or societies – and invited to submit a self-assessment based on lists of personality characteristics supplied by the authors. On the basis of a 70% response rate – and it should be mentioned in passing that the methodology of such an approach is open to question in terms of the structure of the sample, the social conditions affecting reactions to the testing environment, etc. – the authors conclude that clear personality differences do indeed exist between the owners of different pet types.

Kidd *et al.* (1983) describe horse owners as demanding, self-centred and less interested in close human contact. Male horse owners, in their view, are also trying to live out a kind of 'cowboy' fantasy. Snake owners, according to the authors, are unconventional, unpredictable and enjoy taking risks, while pigeon owners are characterized by rational thinking, reliability, a clear sense of purpose and consideration for their fellow men. The principal personality characteristics of caged bird owners are identified as affection for other people and a desire to establish a large number of harmonious interpersonal relationships. Female owners of cage birds are also described by Kidd *et al.* (1983) as 'dominant'.

The study further showed that owners of pigeons and snakes have a special 'scientific interest' in their pets, while owners of horses and caged birds are more concerned with the aspects of communication and companionship between pet and owner.

In an earlier study of cat and dog owners who described themselves as 'lovers' of their preferred pet type, Kidd and Kidd (1980) similarly concluded that pet preferences are linked to differences in biographical data and personality characteristics. Pet owners were analysed in terms of 'autonomy', 'dominance', 'helpfulness' and 'aggression' – four of the basic human needs identified by Murray, and measured here by means of the Edwards' Personality Preference Schedule (Edwards, 1959).

'Autonomy' is understood here as the freedom to come and go as and when one chooses, to be independent of the decisions of others, and to do what one wants without worrying about what other people think. 'Dominance' embraces other aspects of behaviour, such as standing up for one's own point of view, being the leader within a group, always persuading and influencing others, as well as supervising – and controlling – their actions. 'Helpfulness' connotes such things as helping out friends in trouble, treating others in a friendly and sympathetic manner, forgiving their mistakes and gladly doing them a favour, showing affection and seeking to win the confidence of others. 'Aggression', finally, is interpreted as meaning that one never accepts other people's views but always attacks them; that one always blames others whenever anything goes wrong; that one is quick to criticize and insult one's fellow men openly in front of others and that one always finds reasons to justify one's own behaviour, however aggressive (cf. Murray, 1938).

For the purposes of the study, pet owners were categorized as 'dog lovers' or 'cat lovers' on the basis of self-classification. Subjects were also categorized according to sex. Notable among the findings was the fact that female pet owners scored significantly below the average on 'autonomy', while male cat lovers recorded significantly higher scores in this area. Female cat lovers also scored lower on 'dominance' than other subject groups. Cat lovers in general scored significantly lower on 'helpfulness', while female pet owners scored significantly higher. Scores for 'aggression' were lower in the case of female dog and cat lovers, but higher for male dog lovers. It also emerged that cat lovers were significantly less fond of children and adults than dog lovers were.

Findings such as these naturally provoke a certain amount of speculation, not least when considered in relation to other – primarily biographical – data. Thus Kidd and Kidd (1980) were able to show that the predilection for dogs or cats had its roots in childhood, inasmuch as dog lovers kept fewer cats as children, while cat lovers kept fewer dogs.

It has already been shown that there is a positive correlation between the characteristics people ascribe to themselves and the characteristics they ascribe to their pets. Kidd and Kidd (1980) also address themselves to this phenomenon. They noticed, for example, a high degree of correlation between the independence ascribed to a cat and the high scores achieved by cat lovers on the 'autonomy' scale. By comparison, persons who had grown up with dogs and described themselves as dog lovers at the time of the study were more appropriately characterized as 'dominant' and 'aggressive'.

According to the authors, this suggests it is reasonable to assume that lovers of a particular pet type have in many cases grown up in an environment where that kind of psychological correlation between humans and animals existed. This has influenced the development of their own personality – and hence their subsequent preference for a particular pet type.

It is undoubtedly correct to view any correlations that may exist between dog and master as the result of a two-way process and a mutual dependency. It is not only humans who influence dogs: humans are also influenced *by* dogs. The published literature, with its one-sided emphasis on the psychology of human personality, has largely ignored this aspect of mutual dependency – with its attendant behavioural consequences. It should be pointed out, however, that 'dog owners' do not compose a psychologically homogeneous group. Their behaviour reveals individual idiosyn-crasies – not least in their behaviour towards dogs. Lee (1976; cited after Mugford, 1980) divides dog owners into two groups: those who take an *active* interest in their dog and engage in regular play with him, and those who adopt a more passive attitude towards their pet. Only the first group scored higher than non dog owners on affection for other people ('affiliation'). According to Lee, this indicates that dogs are sometimes kept by persons who are in-capable of satisfying all their social needs through interpersonal relationships.

The theoretical basis for Lee's 1976 study was the motivational system formulated by Argyle (1972). This assumes that people are motivated by a number of social drives – hunger, thirst, sexuality, aggression, dependency, affiliation, dominance and self-esteem – as well as various cultural incentives such as success, money, ideology, moral codes, etc. From what has been said already it will be readily apparent that different studies are based on widely differing sets of personality characteristics and modes of self-description. Consequently we are not presented with a coherent personality profile of the 'typical' dog owner. To the extent that the determining characteristics are chosen at random, the resulting 'type' is also a random product. Such results are unsatisfactory from a scientific point of view. A more broadly based approach is required, drawing on the full resources of social psychology and examining a whole range of interactions and reciprocal effects, communication processes and correlations, in order to construct a more subtle and meaningful explanation of pet ownership. It then becomes necessary (for example) to examine the relationship not only between owner and pet, but also between the owner and his fellow human beings. Martinez and Kidd (1980) looked at this area in a study based on the California Psychological Inventory scale for measuring 'well-being' – i.e. the extent to which a person is free from constant self-doubt, feelings of personal insecurity, fears and unrealistic aspirations. They found that the higher scores for well-being were attributable essentially to the specific quality of the individual's personal and social situation – and *not* to ownership of a dog or to the specific quality (in the case of dog owners) of the man–dog relationship.

The existence of studies that reveal no differences between dog owners and non-owners is explained by Martinez and Kidd (1980) in terms of the particular sampling methods used. Thus they are critical of samples selected through the agency of vets and dog shows (see also Kidd and Kidd, 1980), on the grounds that most of the owners approached are persons for whom dog ownership is by definition an important part of life. For their study the authors used the Self-Acceptance Scale from the California Psychological Inventory (cf. Gough, 1975). This is a widely used and comprehensive personality test, which differs from many other test procedures in that it is based not on factor analysis, but on an evaluation of personality structures in terms of plausibility. It consists of 18 rating scales designed to measure a range of personality variables, including dominance, sociability, self-acceptance, general well-being, responsibility, flexibility and femininity. The application of this test to the sample group failed to reveal any obvious differences between dog owners and non-owners.

In another piece of research Kidd and Feldmann (1981) studied a mixed sample of 104 pet owners and non pet owners aged between 65 and 87, using the self-report personality inventory devised by Gough and Heilbrun (1965). The findings show that pet owners are significantly more contented, helpful, optimistic and self-sufficient, while non-owners are less inclined to respect themselves and more inclined to pessimism, dependency on others and self-centredness. In the absence of any control data for other age groups, the validity of these findings is clearly limited. But it does enable us to formulate further hypotheses about the possible age-specific role of animals in the lives of persons living under a variety of different social circumstances. It seems reasonable to assume, for example, that in the case of children and adolescents a dog might satisfy the need for companionship, play, cuddling, fun and amusement, while the elderly look to a dog for other needs – not only companionship, but also therapy, personal protection and a structuring of their daily routine.

A further contribution to the psychological differentiation of pet owners and non-owners is the study by Hyde, Kurdek and Larson (1969), based on a sample whose mean age was 20. Using Hogan's 'empathy scale' (1969) and Rotter's scale for measuring 'interpersonal trust', the authors found very marked differences between pet owners and non-owners. The former scored more highly on 'sense of duty', 'responsibility' and 'leadership qualities', as well as on 'trust in parents, teachers and public figures'.

Given the innate conservatism of the scientific community – that is the general reluctance to deviate from familiar paths of research and experiment with new research models – the various studies cited here will undoubtedly be followed by many more, all of equally dubious value. Quite apart from their lack of comparability in terms of research methods and sampling, all these studies fail to offer an adequate explanation of pet ownership in general and dog ownership in particular because virutally no attempt is made to place them within a broader theoretical context. The authors have resorted instead to arbitrary check-lists of personality traits, in terms of which pet owners and dog owners 'differ' from non pet owners and cat owners – or not, as the case may be.

To recapitulate, the main criticisms of this approach may be summarized as follows:

- The absence of a general theoretical framework, which means that the findings amount to no more than a collection of discrete data which fail to yield any clear overall picture.
- The failure of the various studies to focus clearly on ownership or non-ownership of a dog.
- Methodological weaknesses in the design of certain studies and the testing of hypotheses.

Finally, mention should be made of two aspects that have been virtually ignored by empirical research to date. These are:

1. the motivation underlying the acquisition of a particular type of thoroughbred dog (or indeed a mongrel) and
2. the origins and impact of fashionable trends on the choice of a dog.

Goodwin (1975) and Beck (1975) have pointed out that the number of large dogs in Britain and the USA increased by 10% in the period between 1963 and the early 1970s. In order to document such changing preferences with any certainty, however, it would be necessary to carry out repeat studies over a period of time.

4   The role of dogs in prophylaxis and therapy

The role of dogs in psychiatry and psychotherapy with adolescents and adults

As long ago as the 18th century, it seems, there was a clinic which used 'rabbits and fowls' as instruments of therapy to help patients develop their self-control and accept responsibility (Brickel, 1980). There have since been many other isolated instances of pets being used to develop patients' communication skills and strengthen their hold on reality. But even today we have yet to see the systematic and controlled use of dogs as 'co-therapists'. In order to realize the full potential of animals in the therapeutic process, more interdisciplinary research is needed, with contributions from medical practitioners, psychologists and behavioural scientists.

Most of the publications in this field continue to ignore the 'normal' everyday psychological relationship between humans and dogs (i.e. what dogs mean to people in general and their psychological function for people on a day-to-day basis) in order to focus on the strictly therapeutic aspects. They deal typically with the use of dogs in therapy for the mentally ill, the elderly, children, patients suffering from cardiovascular diseases, and prison inmates.

It is certainly interesting to read in Aschaffenberg (1966; cited after Kidd and Kidd, 1980) that both Freud and Sullivan always kept a dog in their surgery – although we are not told whether these animals played any part in the therapeutic process. Meanwhile Levinson (1972) reports that 33% of the clinical psychologists in New York State use pets as aids to therapy, with dogs as the preferred pet type.

The specific characteristics that make dogs so suitable for use in therapy have been defined by Corson and Corson (1980) as their constant willingness to give affection and tactile contact at all times and in all situations, together with that 'innocent, child-like' trust which dogs unfailingly display towards humans. This reliance on the part of dogs elicits a reciprocal response from humans, who are prepared to put their trust in a dog – and to feel responsible for the animal (see also Siegel, 1962; 1964).

Corson and Corson (1980) and Corson *et al*. (1977) emphasize the special importance in this context of non-verbal communication. The importance of such communication for the regulation of interpersonal behaviour has been amply documented. It has also been shown that the imposition of restrictions on non-verbal contact between humans – as when eye-contact between individuals is impeded by (for example) the wearing of sunglasses – can produce strong feelings of insecurity. To that extent, non-verbal contact is invested with an existential significance (cf. Bergler and Six, 1979; Bergler, 1982). This is no less true, of course, in therapy situations. As Corson and Corson (1980) point out, not enough attention has been paid hitherto to the possibly damaging effects of the non-verbal signals transmitted by the therapist. If a mentally distressed patient receives negative non-verbal signals, this may further aggravate his or her behavioural problems – and perhaps trigger off a vicious circle of mistrust, self-doubt, suspicion and social isolation.

In order to minimize the impact of such (normally involuntary) negative non-verbal signals, the authors recommend the use of dogs as co-therapists. In effect, they assume that communication between dogs and humans is far less likely to break down than communication between humans and their own kind. Dogs are often the object of the patient's own fantasies, needs and longings: and through the 'language' of its eyes, face and body the dog comes to be seen as a partner – an interlocutor – who is totally 'open' and 'honest', without rational design (and therefore without ulterior motive). The problems that can arise in communication between humans are minimized or obviated altogether in communication between humans and dogs. In other words, the crucial, non-verbal process of communication generates trust, confidence, assurance and enhanced self-esteem – and by the same token dispels suspicion, shyness, any tendency to social isolation and diminished self-respect. An awareness of the existential significance of non-verbal communication in human development – stroking, touching, eye-contact, mimicry, gesticulation, pantomime, etc. – has led initially to the use of dogs as co-therapists in a psychiatric clinic in cases of deficient or non-existent communicative skills or a refusal to communicate (Corson and Corson, 1980).

Corson *et al*. (1975a; 1975b; 1977; 1978; 1980) have published a whole series of studies on the use of dogs in psychotherapy in various psychiatric institutes. The authors are careful to point out that 'pet-facilitated psychotherapy' (or PFP) is designed to supplement, and not replace, other forms of psychotherapy. It is a tool to assist the psychotherapeutic process, and an important source of support in the process of resocialization. The success of pet-facilitated psychotherapy is measured by the fact that patients often accept 'love' from a dog (or indeed any other type of pet) more readily and more easily than from other humans. In this 'natural' association with a dog the authors see an explanation for the observable increase in the patient's sense of responsibility, self-assurance and self-esteem. Pet-facilitated psychotherapy is regarded as a form of 'reality conditioning'. Not only is the patient's own self-esteem enhanced and stabilized through regular interaction with the animal and its reactions, but he is also made aware of the limitations on his own behaviour and the modalities of mutual dependency.

Although the authors (Corson *et al*.) say that a pet chosen as co-therapist should be selected according to the particular nature of the mental disturbance and the particular circumstances of the patient, we do not know enough about the mechanisms involved to make that determination. The fact is that much of what passes for psychotherapy still dervies from subjective notions of plausibility, and is an expression of the therapist's own theoretical position and powers of imagination. Corson *et al*. strongly favour the use of dogs in therapy. Among the advantages, in their view, are the wide selection of available breeds (offering a variety of sizes and behavioural patterns) and the large repertoire of reactions that dogs are able to display.

We shall now endeavour to illustrate the general *modus operandi* adopted by Corson *et al*. in pet-facilitated psychotherapy through a number of concrete examples.

The initial contact with the dog took place either at the patient's bedside or at the animal's cage, depending on the degree of rejection or withdrawal exhibited by the patient. As far as possible these encounters were recorded on video, and the recordings were repeatedly played back to the patient. The authors report very rapid initial successes. Young patients began to talk to other children again, asked if they could see the dogs more often – and even asked if they could help with the work of looking after the animals.

As the patient grew accustomed to associating with the dog, his radius of movement became progressively enlarged. In some cases patients were able to move freely about the clinic with their dog, often striking up a conversation about the dog with the people they met, particularly other patients (the dog as social catalyst). And when they were discharged from the clinic, patients were given the option of taking their dog home with them.

The relations and interaction between patient and dog were recorded on video, as was the behaviour of these patients vis-à-vis other patients. A purely quantitative evaluation of the video material revealed that patients were invariably more immediate, direct – more 'normal', in fact – in their verbal reactions both to the dog and to other people (reduction in latency of response). There was also an increase in the number of words used per response, while latterly patients were responding every time to questions put to them by others.

Corson *et al.* used pet-facilitated psychotherapy primarily in the case of patients who had failed to respond to all other forms of therapy. The patients in question were highly introverted, extremely reluctant to make any contact with other people, and in some cases almost dumb. Of the 50 patients treated in this way, only three failed to show any improvement – and in their case no improvement was possible, since they refused to accept the pet. The remaining 47 gradually developed feelings of self-esteem, a desire for independence and a sense of responsibility, and these feelings were strengthened in direct proportion to the degree of care and responsibility assumed by the patient for the care of his dog.

Three case studies provide an illuminating insight into the general progress made in therapy with the various patients:

Case study 1: Randy

Randy was a 13-year-old boy who, after a series of exhibitionistic acts, was admitted to a psychiatric hospital. His behaviour during hospitalization was generally shy and withdrawn, interspersed with occasional scenes of 'clowning'. While undergoing treatment Randy left the hospital on two occasions and went to the nearby university campus, where he exposed himself to female students. The reason for this behaviour was his supposed rejection by the therapist, who had come into the department to play with the patients and had given the impression of favouring another boy over him (Randy). A second incident occurred during a transition period between therapists. Following this incident Randy was forbidden to leave the department unaccompanied.

At the end of six months in hospital Randy had made very little progress. A course of family therapy had also proved unsuccessful. A second therapist was consulted, but he too could see no prospects for a successful cure. Since Randy showed himself co-operative enough in his day-to-day behaviour, the rules formally gave him the freedom to come and go as he pleased. This meant that Randy was in the anomalous position of enjoying certain rights and freedoms in theory, but not being allowed to exercise them in practice because of his supposed exhibitionistic tendencies. The other patients were not aware of the reasons why Randy was forbidden to go out. Under these circumstances Randy got up to some kind of mischief every day. But he stopped behaving like this as soon as he was reprimanded or threatened with punishment.

At this point pet-facilitated psychotherapy was introduced, more or less as a last resort, in an attempt to cure him of his compulsive behaviour. He was now allowed to leave the hospital, unsupervised, for an hour each day, accompanied only by a dog. There was an immediate and dramatic improvement in Randy's behaviour. Staff and patients now found him co-operative, friendly and much more open. He became a serious and responsible partner in the daily therapeutic process – until he had to be discharged from the hospital a month later because of inadequate funding.

Case study 2: Sonny

Sonny was a 19-year-old patient who was suffering from psychotic depression and spent all his time in bed. The staff at the clinic tried to interest him in various activities, but without success. Nothing held any interest for him. He refused to participate in occupational therapy, nor would he take part in relaxation therapy or group therapy sessions. In individual therapy he remained withdrawn and showed no inclination to communicate with others, while behavioural therapy also failed to yield any positive results. Medication was also tried, but his condition showed no improvement. Preparations were therefore made for a course of EST (electroshock therapy). But before this it was decided to try using a dog in the role of co-therapist.

The patient lay in bed as usual in his customary rigid, mummy-like pose. The psychiatrist sat beside him and talked to him. If the psychiatrist's questions were about other people or Sonny himself, his reactions were invariably very slow. But as soon as the questions moved on to the subject of dogs ('Do you like dogs?') or animals in general, he responded much more quickly. Furthermore, Sonny's replies were invariably very brief, usually nothing more than 'yes', 'no' or 'I don't know'. He was not prepared to explain or elaborate or ask questions in his turn. But when the psychiatrist brought a wire-haired fox terrier to Sonny's bedside, Sonny sat up quite spontaneously and took an obvious delight in the dog's friendly behaviour. He immediately became engrossed in the dog, stroking it and talking to it. Very soon the patient was asking 'Where can I keep the dog around here?' No sooner had he said this than the dog ran out into the hall. Sonny promptly ran out after the dog – which was a total break with his previous pattern of behaviour. His behaviour towards other people also changed from this point on. Sonny finally began to take note of other patients, and he now began to attend group therapy sessions. When he was discharged from the clinic his condition was much improved. According to the doctor who was treating him, the dog was the main contributory factor in his recovery.

Case study 3: Marsha

Marsha was a 23-year-old nurse who was admitted to hospital suffering from catatonic schizophrenia. It was impossible to communicate with the patient, who was very restricted in her range of movements and tormented by delusions. Under the influence of her delusions she kept on reiterating her demand that the world should be destroyed. She was treated with drugs, then underwent a course of 24 electroshock treatments. However, no real success was achieved with either of these methods. The patient remained unwilling and unable to make contact with others. It was therefore decided to introduce pet-facilitated psychotherapy into her course of treatment. To begin with, Marsha's behaviour showed no change. But gradually she began to show an interest in the dog, even taking him out for walks. In time she began to stroke the dog as well. Eventually she was given a list of the times when she could see the dog. She began to look forward more and more to these times – and even began to talk to the other patients about the dog. Only six days after the introduction of the dog as co-therapist, Marsha showed a dramatic improvement in her whole pattern of behaviour. Before long she was able to leave the hospital with a positive prognosis.

Theoretical explanations of successful therapies based on the use of pets are still at a very rudimentary stage. In addition to the psychoanalytical interpretations already referred to (Sherick, 1981; De Viney, Dickert and Lockwood, 1983), Brickel (1982) has put forward a theory which essentially relates the positive effects of a pet in psychotherapeutic treatment to an 'attention shift'. In other words, the dog diverts the patient's attention to other elements within an intrinsically critical situation, thereby diminishing the probability that undesirable behaviour will occur. A possible anxiety reaction in a critical situation is rendered less likely by the patient's growing interest in the dog. At the present time it is not possible to say which types of pet in general – and which breeds of dog in particular – are most appropriate for any given diagnosis.

There is no doubt that the use of pets in therapy can assist the process of resocialization. They can act as a link between the patient and everyday reality, divert attention from negative factors, and in the end become a part of the patient's life – and hence of his or her personality (see also Doyle, 1976).

It should be pointed out, however, that under unfavourable personal circumstances, or where there is persistent mental frustration, the patient may become pathologically attached to an animal (Rynearson, 1978). There have also been cases where the death of a beloved pet has been attended by psychopathological consequences. Thus Keddie (1977) describes a case of severe reactive depression in a woman with no previous history of psychiatric disorder, who had kept a dog for 13 years. The condition was, however, successfully treated.

The role of dogs in child therapy

It has already been pointed out that Levinson (1962, 1964, 1965, 1969, 1970, 1972, 1975, 1980) was one of the first to study the psychology of the relationship between pets and humans. One of his primary concerns has been to research the use of pets in child therapy. This form of therapy is felt to be particularly appropriate in cases where the indicated diagnosis is a perceptual, experiential or behavioural disorder rooted in a lack of emotional security during the child's early development. As Levinson points out, the important difference between playing with an animal and playing with dolls or other toys is that the child soon becomes aware of the fact that his feelings are reciprocated. Levinson himself has worked mainly with dogs. He has used them both in the setting of the therapist's surgery and in the patient's own home; in the latter case additional therapy sessions for the child and members of the family have been arranged at the surgery or in the patient's home. Levinson has analysed the successive stages of the therapeutic process as follows.

When the child is first brought to the therapist's surgery by his parents, he is introduced to the therapist and his dog. Normally the child shows an immediate interest in the dog. The ensuing therapeutic process can be broadly divided into two stages (although a clear-cut distinction between the two is not always possible):

1. to begin with, the child plays with the dog, ignoring the therapist.
2. the therapist is then gradually drawn into the interaction between child and dog, while the child's desire to play with the dog fades more and more into the background, until the main focus of attention shifts to the interaction between child and therapist.

Through his relationship with the dog the child thus gains valuable emotional support. He develops confidence in the dog – and hence confidence in himself. Making contact with other people – in this case the therapist – becomes much easier: and this is the necessary first step towards freeing the patient from his neuroses. Once the therapy has progressed to this point, there is every chance that the child will eventually be able to relate to experiences *outside* the therapeutic sessions in an equally well-adjusted manner (Levinson, 1970).

In the alternative procedure for pet-facilitated psychotherapy suggested by Levinson, the pet is introduced into the patient's home and additional therapy sessions are arranged for the child and members of the family. Normally these are also held at the patient's home. Levinson emphasizes that the introduction of a pet into the family home requires careful preparation. To take one example: the child should not be *forced* into looking after the animal. The research findings indicate that the child will *volunteer* to do so as and when he is ready. But if the child views the animal as an extra burden which he is being pressured to take on by his parents, this may well serve to aggravate his emotional conflicts. The pet should not place any additional constraints on the child: on the contrary, its role is to create more 'free space' for the child to develop his own individuality.

To illustrate his procedure Levinson (1970) repeatedly cites case studies. The psychoanalytical nature of his approach is readily apparent, as when he says that the function of a dog should be to give a child pure pleasure – and not to impose constraints like some kind of super-ego. Levinson thus regards animals as an integral part of human social life, but offers no systematic or theoretical discussion of their status. The actual reasons *why* an animal is able to assume the role of co-therapist are not subjected to further critical analysis. While the credit for introducing pets into child therapy undoubtedly belongs to Levinson, whose creative idea it was, his work ultimately remains a blend of subjective plausibility theories with basic psychoanalytical models of human development. If the basic premise underlying this approach is accepted, then of course psychoanalysts, for their part, see no problem about applying this pattern of interpretation to the entire spectrum of possible human behaviours.

The potential value of using dogs in therapy with children has subsequently been acknowledged by other authors besides Levinson. Kusnetzoff (1982) reports on the role played by a dog in therapy with an adolescent for whom the parental home was a source of identification conflicts. Sherick (1981) also emphasizes the therapeutic value of dogs in the treatment of children who have had difficulty in freeing themselves from their mothers and becoming emotionally self-sufficient. Frith (1982) was able to show that dogs and cats help handicapped children to experience feelings of emotional attachment and fulfilment. At the same time, association with a pet broadened their range of interests and enhanced their capabilities. In a more general way, and without adducing any empirical evidence, Teutsch (1980) also notes the importance of pets in therapy with behaviourally disturbed children, emphasizing the need for closer co-operation between medical practitioners, behavioural scientists, psychologists and teachers.

Because the separation of a child from 'his' pet can generate strong feelings of frustration, researchers are now looking into the possibility of the child taking his pet with him when he goes to the clinic – depending on the type of pet and the particular circumstances.

The problem of separation assumes more serious proportions when a pet dies. Mahon and Simpson (1977) observed the reactions of children in a kindergarten to the death of their guinea pig. When a new guinea pig was acquired, the children initially refused to accept it or care for it. They were totally preoccupied with the death of 'their' guinea pig. Some of the children felt angry because the pet had 'deserted' them, some of them felt a sense of guilt. It was only when, under the guidance of their teacher, they were able gradually to come to terms with the death of the guinea pig and genuinely mourn for it, that they could accept the new pet and begin to establish a new relationship.

Given appropriate guidance, therefore, the experience of separation from a pet can help a child to a better understanding of death – which may in turn have a positive impact on the subsequent development of his personality.

Certain aspects of the role of pets in the general psychological development of children are touched upon in passing by the authors of the study cited above. The published literature contains isolated theoretical discussions, but otherwise there have been very few empirical studies dealing with pets in general child development (for exceptions, see Chapter 5). The basic therapeutic possibilities of dogs in particular have been demonstrated in connection with neurotic symptoms, parent–child conflicts, communication conflicts, lack of communication skills and symptoms of autism, i.e. the refusal to enter into contact with other people. At the same time there is a need for more systematic research into pet-facilitated therapy under the 'placebo therapy' rubric, based on the theories of interaction and an understanding of the role of the pet as 'co-therapist'. The work done to date has barely begun to explore these issues.

The role of dogs in the therapy and prophylaxis of cardiovascular disorders

The origins of cardiovascular and psychovegetative disorders are bound up with a number of risk factors, including exposure to stress (Schäfer, 1977). High blood pressure, lack of exercise and the absence of suitable opportunities and strategies for dealing positively with stress situations are all risk factors in cardiovascular disease, and this has led to a consideration of the possible role of dogs in the prevention and treatment of such disorders.

Friedmann et al. (1983) based their experiments on the hypothesis that if children are called upon to perform certain tasks, the presence of a dog will cause their blood pressure to rise less than it otherwise would if the dog were not present. Thirty-six children aged between 9 and 16 each took part in a 10-minute study. A two-minute rest period was followed by a test phase, in which the child was asked to read aloud from a children's book. This procedure was repeated for each child, once in the presence of a dog and once with no dog present. It was found that the systolic, diastolic and central blood pressure (which were measured at one-minute intervals) and the pulse rate were significantly lower when the dog was present than when it was absent. The authors concluded that a dog is able to exercise a calming influence in a situation that generates fear or stress. In short, the dog has an 'anti-stress effect'. We do not yet know what mechanisms are at work here. It may be that the presence of a dog somehow 'defuses' the whole situation. It may also be that non-verbal communication between dog and child creates in the latter a feeling of security and self-confidence.

Katcher (1979) also found that hypertensives experienced a drop in blood pressure whenever they stroked a small dog or looked at tropical fish in an aquarium. As soon as they entered into conversation with another person, however, their blood pressure rose to its original level.

It is reasonable to postulate, therefore, that physiological excitement which is the expression of stress in any form can be reduced by the presence of a dog or other animal – as indeed can the patient's general susceptibility to illness (Thurlow, 1967). It is interesting to note in this connection that pulse rate and blood pressure in dogs and horses both show a significant fall when these animals are stroked by humans (Anderson and Gantt, 1966; Lynch and McCarthy, 1969, 1977; Lynch et al., 1974; Newton and Ehrlich, 1966). We do not appear to have any data as yet that would indicate whether or not corresponding physiological reactions also occur in the person who is stroking the animal.

Good results have also been achieved with the aid of dogs in the aftercare of angina pectoris and cardiac infarcts. For example, Katcher (1979) found that victims of angina pectoris or a cardiac infarct had a 400% better chance of survival if they owned a pet. This difference between pet owners and non-owners remained significant even when dog owners were excluded and allowance was made both for the gravity of the attack and for whether or not the victim's own partner was still alive. Dog owners were excluded because it was felt they might show a higher degree of physical fitness (perhaps as a result of walking their dog), which would then distort the findings. The decisive factor here, of course, is the anti-stress effect which the pet has on its owner. If we accept the distinction betwen 'Type A' persons (Friedmann and Rosemann, 1975) (i.e. people who feel in a constant state of stress which they believe themselves powerless to resist) and 'Type B' persons (i.e. people who take everything in their stride in a more relaxed and easy fashion) then the theory assumes that Type A persons carry a higher risk of infarction than Type B persons (Zimmerman, 1982). Katcher (1979) argues that association with an animal, especially a dog, could induce a Type A person to adopt a pattern of behaviour more akin to that of a Type B. This in turn would increase that person's resistance to stress and lower the risk of infarction. The questions raised by such a typology of personality, both in terms of its theoretical basis and its diagnosis, are beyond the scope of the present discussion.

It is interesting to note, in connection with the possible role of dogs in therapy and communication, that something like 50% of patients who had suffered a cardiac infarct also had chronic family difficulties and virtually no social contacts outside the family.

Friedmann's 1983 study starts from the general proposition that pets have a positive effect on a person's state of health. Like Katcher before her, Friedmann looked at the chances for survival of patients suffering from coronary artery disease. She found that a survival period of one and a half years following a cardiac infarct was significantly more frequent among pet owners than among non-owners. This encouraging pattern of rehabilitation was explained with reference to pet ownership in 23.5% of cases (after allowing for variance). The specific benefits of pet ownership in this instance were identified as the regular physical exercise associated with keeping a dog, and a relatively continuous and stress-free communication situation.

Despite these findings, Friedmann (1983) could not provide satisfactory proof of the existence of a direct cause-and-effect relationship between dog ownership and health status. In order to establish such a link, other possible causal factors – such as personality type, socio-economic status, quality and quantity of social relations, etc. – would have to be taken into account. The doubts that remain as to the precise nature of the relationship, causal or otherwise, are attributed by the author to a dearth of research into the character of the relationship between 'normal' humans and 'normal' animals, as well as to a lack of knowledge about the concrete effects on human health of cohabitation with animals.

Although there undoubtedly are major gaps in our research knowledge, the role of dogs as aids to therapy and prophylaxis in medical practice is being increasingly acknowledged – not least in West Germany. A 1983 survey of West German medical practitioners showed that 54% of the 100 doctors interviewed had recommended to at least one of their patients that he or she should acquire a dog (see MAFO Institute, 1983). Most of these doctors also believed that by following this advice their patients could bring about a marked improvement in their condition, as indicated below:

- Cardiovascular diseases, circulatory disorders   48%
- Depression   46%
- Loneliness, isolation   33%
- Obesity   28%
- Lack of exercise (general)   19%
- High blood pressure   9%
- Diseases of the locomotor system   7%
- Diabetes   4%
- Other conditions   4%

Here we find a recognition of the possible role of a dog in reducing the risk factor 'lack of exercise', as well as in reinforcing a sense of personal well-being – thereby enhancing, ultimately, the individual's own quality of life.

The importance of dogs for the blind

As we have seen, dogs can play an important part in stimulating social interaction and communication. It is not surprising, therefore, that people should have explored the possibility of using dogs to extend the highly restricted social range of the blind, as well as to secure their personal safety in the immediate physical environment.

The work done with the blind has yielded one study of particular interest for our present purposes. Delafield (1976; cited after Mugford, 1980) compared the self-esteem of blind persons with and without a dog. The study is based on the assumption that an individual's self-esteem is dependent on:

(a) the perceived expectations that others have of oneself, i.e. society's expectations;
(b) one's own values, one's expectations of oneself and of society, and one's own self-image;
(c) one's own perception of certain environmental stimuli.

Several different measures of self-esteem were applied. It emerged that blind persons *with* a guide dog esteem themselves more highly than blind persons *without* a dog. In a word, they have more faith in themselves. It is also interesting to note that blind persons experienced a significant boost in self-esteem when they acquired a dog for the first time.

The importance of a dog for a person's own self-confidence and self-esteem – and hence for the assurance and naturalness with which that person relates to other people – becomes especially apparent in a world such as that of the blind, where the possibilities for communication are so very restricted. Inasmuch as the purpose of the present study is to establish whether or not a dog enhances the quality of individual human life, here at least the answer must be overwhelmingly in the affirmative.

5   The role of dogs in developmental psychology

In current scientific thinking, human developmental psychology is properly concerned with the entire course of human life. We speak of developmental psychology in relation to the child and adolescent, but equally in relation to adult life. Research into the role of dogs in developmental psychology has hitherto tended to focus on the two areas of child development and geriatric development (with particular reference to people living alone).

Dogs and children

There is no doubt that humans and animals interact through a wide range of positive and mutually agreeable experiences. Animals play an important role in our everyday lives and in our dreams. Our preferences for certain types of pet are very likely to change in the course of our development, as shown in a study by Salomon (1984). The author put a list of six questions to a sample of 216 boys and girls aged between 5 and 13:

1. What is your favourite animal?
2. Which is your favourite animal among those that live in the wild?
3. What is your favourite pet?
4. If you could choose to be an animal, which animal would you choose to be?
5. Which animals do you dislike and which ones frighten you?
6. Which animals do you see most often in your dreams?

Some of the author's findings are discussed briefly below.

   The first point to emerge was that with only three exceptions *all* the children, regardless of age, wanted to own a pet. However, the preferred pet type did vary according to age, as Table 4 clearly shows.

Table 4 Stated pet preferences among children

Question: What is your favourite animal?	Age Group I (average age 6.5 years)	Age Group II (average age 9.5 years) (%)	Age Group III (average age 11.5 years)
Cat	21.7	30	12.5
Horse	19.5	16	17.5
Dog	17.3	29.9	35
Others	41.5	24.1	35

The figures show that children find dogs more appealing as they grow older. It seems that children do not want to be a dog themselves, however. In response to question 4, most children in Age Group I said 'a cat', while the answers 'bird' or 'horse' were favoured by the older age groups.

Asked which was their favourite wild animal, children in all age groups gave 'lion' and 'tiger' as their first two preferences. Age-related changes in the preference for a particular animal therefore seem to be determined largely by whether or not the animal in question can be integrated within a person's own environment – i.e. whether (amongst other things) the animal can help to satisfy a person's own psychological needs and thus enhance his quality of life through communication and emotional support.

In this context it is interesting to note some of the age-related reasons that are given for various preferences. On the basis of the reasons given by children for preferring certain types of animal,

Table 5 Motives governing the choice of a pet

	Age Group I (average age 6.5 years)	Age Group II (average age 9.5 years) (%)	Age Group III (average age 11.5 years)
Love and security	41.7	18	28.3
Autonomy and independence	23.8	54.5	59.2
Self-assurance and aggression	19.4	23.8	9.8
No classification possible	15.1	3.7	2.7

Salomon (1984, p. 217ff.) divides the motives governing the choice of a pet into three categories (see Table 5).

While rigid phase models of this kind need to be interpreted with caution, based as they are on the assumption that children's experience and behaviour can be divided into a number of distinct phases defined by age, the findings do show that these age-related preferences are also the expression of age-related needs and motivational states. The importance of animals as one possible route to autonomous and relatively independent behaviour and action would appear to increase with age. 'Love and security' are primarily of importance to the youngest age group – although this factor regains something of its significance with the onset of puberty.

This study can only be viewed as the first step towards a full examination of the age-specific significance of pets. The scope of the inquiry would need to be extended to cover all the stages in a person's life. I shall return to this question later in the light of my own research findings.

Most of the studies dealing with the role of dogs in developmental psychology are based on various subjective criteria of plausibility. These would need to be developed into properly founded theoretical hypotheses, which could then be tested by empirical methods. Levinson, for example, has completed several studies into the possible influences of animals on child development, based largely on criteria of plausibility (Levinson, 1972; 1978; 1980). He too assumes that the role of animals is age-specific. Thus a baby learns to distinguish between its mother and other people during the second six months of its first year of life. It is afraid of strangers, cries when its mother is not there, and shows its pleasure when she returns. Children in this situation need a special 'cuddly animal', a soft toy that is always there to act as a bridge between them and the world around them, thereby helping them to develop confidence in that world and in themselves. This animal comes to be seen by the child as a constant source of support and consolation, not least at those times when adults are making their first demands on a child (potty training, etc.) and certain conflicts are unavoidable.

When the child enters school, he is expected to take responsibility for himself, i.e. to develop a measure of independence and the ability to stand on his own two feet. He is more likely to succeed in this if he is able to explore and master hitherto unknown areas of the world around him from a position of independence. If a child is accompanied in his explorations by a dog, he is less likely to be afraid – and his parents feel reassured. If a child is responsible for looking after a dog and training it, he has to accustom himself to the discipline of a fixed routine. And whenever the child succeeds in teaching the dog something, his own self-esteem is boosted, which in turn helps him to deal better with setbacks in other areas of his life.

A child's experience of training a pet also teaches him to accept the animal's individual peculiarities. This can lead to greater tolerance, not least in respect of one's own weaknesses. A géneral acceptance of the animal is often followed by partial identification with it, i.e. the child learns to share the animal's thoughts and feelings. If one loves a pet and wishes to 'read' its feelings in the sounds it makes, in its expression and its behaviour, one has to pay very close attention and endeavour at all times to place oneself in the animal's position. Constant association with a pet also shows a child how his own behaviour affects the animal, and vice versa. A kind of subliminal learning process takes place, as the child comes to understand what it means when living beings can only co-exist in a state of mutual dependency. The sense of being the pet's 'master' can also help the child to feel on a more equal footing with its parents, and to experience a growing feeling of healthy independence (Levinson, 1978, 1980).

At the same time Levinson (1980) points out that the affection, love and sympathy displayed by a child for a pet are not always transferred automatically to the sphere of human relations. In other words, a pet can 'teach' a child to love it, to identify and associate with it, but this does not necessarily mean that the child is able to identify with and understand other human beings. Here the parents must step in and supplement the educational process, encouraging the child to transfer his experiences with the animal to the interpersonal domain.

As he grows older, the child wants to be acknowledged and respected not only within his own family, but also by others outside the family circle. Here a dog can help to facilitate contact with others and secure social recognition for a child.

A pet can also serve as a useful point of reference which parents can use as a basis for discussing difficult problems such as sexuality and the basic facts of life and death. This point has also been made by Crase and Crase (1976), who particularly emphasize the possibility of inculcating in the child an understanding of death as a universal, inevitable and irreversible phenomenon, and helping him to an experience of mourning as a *positive* strategy for dealing with loss ('A child should be allowed to mourn for a pet').

Levinson (1980) believes that pets can also be directly involved in a child's sexual development. A pet can be the medium through which a child learns to witness and comprehend the processes of procreation and birth. At the same time a pet can perform a very useful function when the family moves house – an event which, for the child, normally involves the loss of familiar home surroundings, friends, schoolmates and trusted teachers. In this situation a pet is able to give the child stability and reassurance.

Another difficult situation for a child is the birth of a brother or sister. Suddenly he finds that his parents, relatives and family friends are focusing all their attention on the new-born baby. Once again, the child turns to his pet for much-needed emotional support.

Perhaps the most critical situation for a child arises on the death of, or separation from, one of his parents or siblings. In many cases the remaining parent is unable to provide the affection a child needs, but a pet can serve as a surrogate source of affection.

Wolfe (1977) has published a preliminary empirical study of the 'mediating function' of pets in adolescent relationships. The author is concerned with the role of animals in specific situations where other people in the immediate social environment cannot – or, for whatever reasons, will not – perform this mediating, communicative function, and where such people are not accepted, psychologically, by adolescents. Wolfe's investigations have shown that the 'mediating function' of a pet consists in the way it can satisfy the need for consolation, facilitate adjustment to other people, and help its owner to come to terms with dramatic occurrences. A mediating function is also apparent in the way pets are perceived and experienced as the embodiment of desirable social and personal characteristics, such as friendliness, warmth, constancy, reliability, sympathy and the ability to identify with the feelings of others. In other words, the 'value' of the pet to an adolescent, which is Wolfe's sole concern in this study, consists in the mediation of characteristics that are desirable and necessary for that person's psychological stability. What this mediating function ultimately tells us is that the relationship between humans and pets is one of mutual dependency and communication.

Pets and the elderly

A socially isolated person cannot survive in this world. Human experience and development are the product of mutual dependency between human beings, between humans and animals, and between humans and the forces of nature and civilization. Only if we live in an environment that is both stimulating and challenging can we hope to develop in an active and positive way, thereby exercising a favourable influence on our life expectancy. But mutual stimulation can only conduce to a *positive* end if there is an underlying basis of sympathy and affection: where such positive feelings are absent, human relationships are experienced as a source of stress.

Every person is threatened with increasing social isolation as he or she grows older. Social losses gradually come to outweigh social gains, as a person's network of social contacts dwindles in size and alters in character. These losses are perceived in terms of a comparison with younger people and various reminders that one is getting older: the sight of one's own children growing up, the reduction in the number of one's own roles and positions (work, clubs and societies, parents, grandparents, relations, friends, etc.) and the range of activities available to one within those roles that remain. This process is frequently accompanied by a loss of social power and responsibility, together with a general decline in the quantity and quality of social transactions (Bergler, 1979).

In the light of this developmental profile, it is easy to understand why the situation of old people living alone or in an old people's home should have prompted speculation as to how far the presence of a dog might serve to alleviate certain negative aspects of their life – or indeed turn those aspects to positive advantage. The situation of old people living alone is often associated with growing social isolation and the absence of important tasks or responsibilities. Social isolation is further aggravated by the inadequacy of the financial resources available to many elderly people, by their lack of mobility, their physical frailty, the death of a partner or relatives, friends and peers, the moving-away of children or younger relatives, and the widespread prejudices that exist against the elderly (Bennett, 1973; Thomson, 1973; Bergler, 1979).

Under such circumstances it is not surprising that old people are prone to depression and feelings of helplessness and despair. It is reasonable to assume that a dog might be able to break this vicious circle of social isolation by helping the individual to make new social contacts, adopt a more ordered and regulated life-style, and to be generally more 'reality-orientated' (Walster, 1979; Cusack and Smith, 1984). The purpose of this therapeutic (or at the very least, prophylactic) use of dogs is ultimately to enhance the quality of life enjoyed by elderly people living alone, primarily through a reinforcement of the socio-communicative stimulus, i.e. resocialization.

Walster (1975, p. 15) has summarized the many advantages and benefits of dog ownership for the elderly. He lists the following factors:

Prevention of loneliness
Giving a sense of security
Sociability

A way of helping others:
- taking neighbours' dogs for walks when they are out at work
- looking after school pets in the holidays
- looking after cage birds at weekends

Comparing notes with others: a chance to talk and exchange ideas
Reinforced reality-orientation
Incentive to undertake new activities
Possibility of identifying with other people
Ready-made topic of conversation
Becoming involved with the practical details of dog purchase and ownership, e.g. visits to the pet shop or kennels, vaccinations, health care for the dog, insurances, etc.
Loyal devotion to another living creature
A chance to put one's talents and abilities to good use again
A substitute for other social relationships
A means of sharing a sense of accomplishment with others
Relaxation
A sense of being needed
Loving and being loved

The situation of the elderly in a residential old people's home clearly differs from that of old people living alone at home. In referring to the mental and social milieu of old people's homes, Corson and Corson (1978; 1980) have used terms such as 'isolation', 'depression', 'hopelessness', 'helplessness', 'boredom' and 'low self-esteem'. This can be attributed in large part to the social structure of such institutions. Old people's homes are often geared to the processing of people *en masse*, with few opportunities for individual initiative and the safeguarding of the private sphere. Many residents lose touch with one of the most important driving forces for the maintenance and enrichment of human life, that is meaningful and satisfying activity, activity with a purpose. The environment is often not calculated to foster positive states of mind, nor to give residents the feeling that they are needed, liked and accepted – and able to reciprocate such feelings. Most resi-

dents are deprived of the tactile contact that supports social relations, and progressive deterioration of the sense organs increases
tactile and social isolation. The end result is a vicious circle, where
increasing social isolation fuels mental and emotional disintegration and disorientation and vice versa (Corson and Corson, 1978,
1980).

Animals offer one way out of this vicious circle. Brickel (1979)
has described a study he carried out with cats in an old people's
home. The introduction of the cats led to an increase in the residents' receptivity to various external stimuli, such as the lobby fur-
nishings, other residents, the nurses, etc. The animals were viewed
as companions, and some of the patients took great pleasure in
looking after them. They gave a lot of joy and satisfaction to the old
people in the home, and the presence of the animals seemed to
generate a cosy, domestic sort of atmosphere. In general it was
observed that the old people became more attuned to the reality
around them, they began to have more contact with other people
again, they took more interest in their surroundings and found
their bearings more easily.

Corson and Corson (1978, 1980) did a study with dogs in an old
people's home which led them to very similar findings. The case
study cited below gives a graphic insight into the kind of
behavioural changes that occurred.

Case study: Jed

Jed was in his late seventies and had been living for the past 26 years in
a nursing home. He had been admitted to the 'Castle Nursing Homes'
in Millesburg, Ohio, in 1949, after falling from a tower and suffering
brain damage. At the time of his admission he was thought to be deaf
– also as a result of his accident.

During the years that followed Jed was unsociable and inattentive.
Staff were able to communicate with him only by hand signals. Since
Jed was able to read, his nurse wrote him notes to discover his needs
and wishes. He himself was unable to communicate intelligibly with
others through the spoken word. He spent most of his time just sitting
around in silence. Occasionally he would mutter unintelligibly to
himself.

This went on until the director of the nursing home, Donald De
Haas, introduced Jed to the dog Whisky. This produced a totally
unexpected spontaneous reaction from Jed, who spoke a complete
sentence for the first time in 26 years: 'You've brought me this dog.' Jed
fondled the dog and took great delight in it. Jed now began to talk to
staff members about 'his' dog; his powers of communication – and his
willingness to communicate – were increasingly restored. The nurses

also noticed an improvement in his general condition and his inter-personal behaviour. He also began, quite spontaneously, to draw pictures of dogs. And the more pictures of dogs he drew, the more individual and 'personalized' they became in terms of details such as teeth, claws, etc.

Later on Jed was also introduced to Fluff, a lively wire-haired fox terrier. Jed quickly made friends with this dog too, and announced: 'I'm going to take care of you.' Which he did – and the two became inseparable friends.

In this case pet-facilitated psychotherapy undoubtedly helped the patient to re-establish contact with his fellow human beings, and, increasingly, to recover his ability to communicate intelligibly through the spoken word. Jed now took great pains to make himself understood, particularly when talking about his dog.

In her 1981 study Blake likewise examined the effects of contact with a pet on the residents of an old people's home. She started from the general hypothesis that under these conditions pets would have a positive influence on the general mental disposition, self-confidence, self-esteem and indeed the socialization of the elderly. In this study the old people were able to select their own pets. For the first few weeks the presence of the pets did create certain difficulties in the home. Five weeks after their introduction, however, Blake reports that a very definite normalization took place. The author views her study as a pilot project, which by and large confirms her initial hypotheses.

In England, Mugford and M'Cominsky (1975) carried out another study with elderly people in which the latter were given either a budgerigar or a houseplant to keep in their room. Those who opted for a budgerigar developed a 'surprisingly intimate rapport' with the creature. The new relationship with a pet also meant that the old people were once again able to engage in lengthy conversations with other people. Hitherto the dominant topic of conversation had been 'illness': this was now supplanted almost entirely by the patients' constant association with their budgerigars.

Another study, by Andrysco (1982), describes the introduction of a dog into an old people's home and compares the behaviour of people who had constant contact with the dog with the behaviour of a control group living under closely comparable conditions, except for the fact that they could not develop a relationship with an animal. Using video recordings, the study centred around observation of the communicative behaviour of humans and dogs. The general reaction of the old people to the introduction of the dog was very positive, and concomitant changes in interpersonal relations were also observed. There was an increase in eye-contact, smiling, tactile contact, the number of spoken words and the number of questions asked. The findings indicate that the presence of a dog in an old people's home gives the residents increased opportunities for tactile contact and non-verbal communication, thereby contributing significantly to the alleviation of feelings of loneliness, depression and helplessness – which in turn explains the changes in interpersonal behaviour described above.

Andrysco (1982) speaks in this connection of a pet-facilitated 'reality therapy'. Piotrowsky (1984) also described the positive results obtained by other authors when they introduced dogs into old people's homes. In Melbourne, for example, a former guide dog for the blind spent a continuous period of six months with the 60 residents of one such home. This association produced a marked increase in general sociability and an improvement in patient morale. These observations and findings prompted Piotrowsky to raise for consideration the question of whether patients should be permitted, under certain conditions, to take their dogs or other pets with them when they are hospitalized. As Piotrowsky himself notes:

'In nearly 30 years as a practising physician I have come across count-less patients who had a snapshot of their dog on the bedside table. And as soon as the conversation turned to their dog, we were able to estab-lish an instant rapport' (Piotrowsky, 1984, p. 8).

In this context the author (Piotrowsky, 1984) also describes an experiment conducted in Britain under the auspices of the National Health Service, whereby patients who were hospitalized for an extended period were allowed to take their dogs into hospi-tal with them. No long-term findings have yet been published. As far as hygiene is concerned, Piotrowsky sees no real problems with pets that are basically easy to care for. While he is not in favour of *all* patients being allowed to bring their dog into hospital, he does suggest that this possibility should be available for patients with terminal cancer, as a way of raising their spirits and combating the feeling of total isolation.

Dogs, health and hygiene

Although problems of hygiene as such hardly arise any more in connection with dog ownership, they are repeatedly cited by indi-viduals and certain sections of the media as one of the penalties or 'cost factors' of dog ownership. The belief that dogs are carriers of certain diseases is founded on ignorance and prejudice. The fact is that people are far more likely to pick up an infection these days at the local sports club, on the bus or train, or because they are exposed to particular forms of environmental pollution. The same applies to allergies, which are caused by hundreds of substances commonly present in the environment. Unfortunately, dog excrement *has* been shown to pose a threat, in particular to children who may come into contact with toxicana canis when playing in the park (see p. 104).

There is also an aesthetic problem with regard to dog excrement which dog owners themselves could do much to solve.

We are currently engaged in an interdisciplinary research project involving vets and psychologists, with the object of analysing the objective health status of dog owners, possible interactions between dogs and humans and the psychology of dog and cat ownership. On the basis of our findings to date it appears almost certain that the fears commonly expressed on this account are not justified by the facts (Mayr, 1986; Bergler, 1986).

Psychological advantages and disadvantages of dog ownership

Despite the absence of theoretical underpinning, the insufficiently representative nature of the samples, the frequent preoccupation with subjective criteria of plausibility and a methodology that sometimes leaves much to be desired, the body of scientific work reviewed in these pages has demonstrated very clearly that the relationship between man and dog is an extremely important – as well as interesting – area of research. As the relationship between man and his pets has gradually ceased to be taken for granted as something natural, the many symptoms of a new 'unnatural' lifestyle, with its attendant breakdowns in interpersonal relations, have prompted scientific observers to ask what role pets in general – and dogs in particular – might be able to play in a human life. To answer this question is *ipso facto* to identify the motives that prompt a person to acquire a dog or not, as the case may be.

Once we have empirical evidence to show what a dog means to people in different situations, different age groups and different states of physical and mental health, we are in a position to define the nature of the relationship between dogs and the quality of human life. The psychological benefits of dog ownership can be measured in terms of the needs that a dog is able to satisfy, albeit the process is one of interaction, not to say mutual dependency. These benefits must then be offset against the psychological *costs* of dog ownership. After taking account in this way of all the plus and minus factors, we should be able to define the dog's contribution to human well-being with some degree of accuracy. That at least is the theoretical basis for the present study and in the pages that follow we shall briefly summarize the results of previous research into this particular aspect.

'Quality of life' is a subjective concept. One person may find a pet essential to his well-being, while to another a pet would be an intolerable burden that detracts considerably from the quality of life.

Quality of life, as perceived by the individual, is largely a matter of one's general satisfaction with life. This in turn is based on the degree of satisfaction gained in many different areas of life, and the importance or centrality of those areas to the individual concerned. For some, pet ownership is one such area of central importance. The decision whether to acquire a pet or not – and if so, what sort – is largely governed by individual perceptions of the costs and benefits of pet ownership. Now 'costs' and 'benefits' are to be understood very largely in psychological terms, i.e. in terms of experiences, ideas, the pros and cons that we associate, consciously or unconsciously, with pet ownership. And since even pet owners recognize the disadvantages of pet ownership, it is ultimately a question of weighing up the respective costs and benefits and making a qualitative judgement.

An understanding of the specific motivational states of dog owners and non-owners furnishes a useful point of departure for the interpretation, prognosis and modification of human behavioural patterns. It is important to recognize that human behaviour is not triggered by what is factually, objectively 'the case', but by our subjective perceptions of reality, i.e. the significance that we choose to ascribe to people, things, animals and relational structures. There is a further difficulty here, in that a decision may be taken in a given situation *without* a knowledge of all the factors involved. Mugford (1980) points out that the functions associated with dog ownership have changed as a result of such broad social trends as industrialization, urbanization, the supplanting of the extended family by the nuclear family, the declining birth rate in heavily industrialized countries, the development of mass communications and mass transportation, better education and a higher level of aspiration, the break-up of the class system, etc. Today the primary emphasis in dog ownership is on the social and communicative aspects, which extend beyond the dog itself to embrace other people. For dogs have an important role as a 'social catalyst'. In a study undertaken in Sweden by Bath *et al.* (1976), 57% of those interviewed claimed that they had made new friends through their dog. Only 5% said that they had actually made enemies through their dog. Other benefits identified by the interviewees include the opportunity to play together, the receiving and giving of love, a sense of security, the dog as a mirror of one's own personality, an expression of self-love (narcissism), the dog as status symbol and the educational value for one's own children. According to the authors, 76% of dog owners said that their dog gave them a 'feeling of security', while no less than 96% said that their dog made them feel 'warm and affectionate'. Sixty per cent of the dog owners in the study claimed that they spent more than half an hour each day playing with their dog.

Ryder (1973) has attempted a general assessment of the benefits of pet ownership, with special reference to dogs. The benefits he lists are:

1. tactile contact which has no sexual connotations and therefore carries no taboo;
2. empathy, i.e. the feeling of being understood and loved by one's pet;
3. a sense of one's own importance;
4. loving and being loved;
5. feelings of closeness to nature;
6. security;
7. the inculcation of socially desirable characteristics;
8. prestige, i.e. the ability to impress others through the dog;
9. having a convenient scapegoat;
10. the experience of power and dependency;
11. sexual stimulation;
12. opportunities for play;
13. the dog as social catalyst (see also Yoxall, 1979; Wilbur, 1976).

Two benefits which are particularly relevant to the use of dogs in therapy – though they are by no means without importance in 'normal' situations outside the therapeutic process – are the feelings of being needed and the enforced adoption of a regular daily routine (see also Walster, 1979).

The cost factors of dog ownership are listed as follows:

1. financial expenditure on food, grooming aids and medical care;
2. restricted freedom of movement;

3. short life span of dogs;
4. complications when the owner becomes ill or dies;
5. problems with hygiene;
6. allergies;
7. transmission of diseases;
8. excessive noise;
9. destruction of own or others' property;
10. aggressive behaviour (see also Walster, 1979, p. 15; Wilbur, 1976).

To define the costs and benefits of dog ownership is *ipso facto* to define the motivation underlying the acquisition of a dog. Zemanek (1981) has studied this 'behavioural propensity' for acquiring a pet. His findings show that attitudes to pet ownership ('pleasant–unpleasant') and to dogs and cats ('agreeable–disagreeable'), the ability to cope with problems on a journey and personal assessments of the time available for a pet are all extremely reliable indicators of future behaviour. It appears that pet owners are significantly less reluctant to accept restrictions on their freedom or to enter into a long-term commitment. Typical attitude profiles of pet owners and non-owners, dog owners and cat owners reveal different attitude structures for each type.

The 'cost/benefit' approach in psychology is based on certain theories about how attitudes function – and here the question of the relationship between attitudes and behaviour is of vital importance (see Chapter 6). In other words, we need a theory and methodology that are capable of explaining and forecasting observable forms of behaviour, such as the ownership or non-ownership of dogs.

General attitudes to, and evaluations of, pets are clearly *not* sufficient as an explanation of concrete behaviour. The same can also be said of the approach adopted (for example) by Templer *et al.* (1981).

We shall conclude by listing once again, in a little more detail in some cases, the various psychological costs and benefits identified by the authors whose work we have reviewed in these pages. The items (see Table 5) are not listed in any order of precedence: we have merely attempted to summarize all the references to the roles, functions and possibilities for gratifying human needs that a dog embodies. It was already clear from our previous findings that the psychological 'utility–function profile' of a dog is determined by a whole series of factors, including the owner's age, family situation, subjective health status and objective clinical picture, past

Table 6 Findings contained in the literature reviewed

Psychological advantages of dog ownership

Sociability, interaction, mutual dependence
Communication, with special reference to non-verbal behaviour
Tactile stimulation and tactile contact
Making contact: the dog as social catalyst; making friends
Warmth, affection, love
Stable, positive reference object
Playmate: shared enjoyment and feelings of togetherness
Physical exercise: change of behaviour; regulation of circulation
Closeness to nature: natural relationships taken for granted
Stress-reducing or stress-free relationships
Security: alleviating feelings of anxiety and diminished self-confidence
The experience of being needed: sympathy and attention
The experience of being understood: someone who listens without
    contradicting
Inculcating self-esteem, self-confidence, self-assurance
The dog as status symbol
A focus for one's own narcissism
A model of socially desirable characteristics
Compensation for one's own failings: stabilization of self-esteem
Self-stabilization in emotional crises
Stabilization of social situations
A part of one's own personality (identification problems)
Enforced adoption of a regular daily routine
Teaching children about central life events: birth, sexuality, death
Dogs as an aid to child development and upbringing: learning about
    responsibility, self-discipline, how to cope with frustration
Therapy for psychological and neurotic symptoms
The dog as scapegoat for one's own maladjusted behaviour

Psychological disadvantages of dog ownership

A source of social conflict: the possibility of dog owners making enemies
Restrictions on personal freedom of movement
Aggressive behaviour towards other people
Problems with one's partner
Damage to property (own and other people's)
Excessive noise
Cost of food, grooming aids and medical care
Problems arising when the owner falls ill or dies
Relatively short life span of dogs
Risk of transmitting disease
Allergies

experiences with pets, exposure to social situations that generate conflict and stress, personal mobility, and the nature and number of social reference persons and social reference groups available to that person. Nor can it be assumed, at this point in time, that these factors are entirely separate and unrelated. More empirical research into the factors themselves – and their possible inter-dependence – is now urgently needed.

In the chapters that follow we shall conduct a psychological investigation into the relationship between dogs, human personal-ity and quality of life via an analysis of the individual's decision to acquire a dog on the basis of the psychological benefits and costs entailed. We are not concerned here with particular groups of per-sons who share a common clinical history, but with a representa-tive sample of the West German population. The only distinctions made are between dog owners, owners of other pets and non pet owners.

6 The psychology of dog ownership: experimental design principles

Theoretical foundations*

Leaving aside one or two psychoanalytical approaches to the problem, our survey of the literature has shown that we still lack a satisfactory scientific explanation of the relationship between man and
dog. Both popular discussion and scientific research have hitherto
confined themselves to certain selected aspects, such as the advantages and disadvantages of dog ownership, or the attempt to discover a correlation between personality traits (including so-called
sociodemographic data – age, occupation, income, etc.) and dog
ownership. The role of dogs in therapy and prophylaxis has also
attracted a good deal of critical discussion. Finally, we have a
whole group of studies that approach the relationship between
man and dog via various criteria of plausibility. The end result is a
mixed bag of discrete findings which need to be put together to
form an overall picture, or theoretical model, that will enable us to
explain and predict the behaviour and experience of dog owners as
a group.

A brief description of the 'motives' that conduce to dog ownership, or the establishment of correlations between certain general
personality traits and dog ownership, cannot suffice to explain the
decision-making processes, value systems and life-styles that cause
a person to acquire a dog. Hence the need to develop a theoretical
model that will explain the psychology of dog ownership, taking
into account the current theoretical trends in social psychology.
Effective research is impossible without a comprehensive
behavioural model of this kind, as a number of studies on market
psychology have shown (Sheth, 1974; Bergler, 1982, 1984).

The present study takes as its starting point the key significance
of attitudes in human perception, orientation and decision making.
Attitudes are an important component both of our intended
actions and of the actions that we actually complete. The values of
any methodology developed on this theoretical basis has to be

*Readers who are not interested in the theoretical principles should turn straight
to Chapter 7 for a discussion of the findings.

measured in terms of how far it is successful in explaining and forecasting specific instances of human behaviour. Two theoretical developments in experimental psychology that have proved particularly fruitful in this regard are expectancy value theories and the theory of exchange.

Expectancy value theories

Originally developed within the context of motivational psychology (see for example Vroom, 1964; Heckhausen, 1977, 1981; Feather, 1982), this theoretical school attributes a significant explanation value to personal expectancy values as they relate to possible objectives in human conduct and behaviour. This approach has been applied with some degree of success in organizational psychology, particularly in terms of explaining job satisfaction, performance motivation, work behaviour and patterns of behaviour within organizations in general (Mitchell, 1974; Wahaba and House, 1974; Weinert, 1981).

In the context of social psychology, 'expectations' are simply attitudes that carry a particular personal and motivational significance. In the broadest sense they are the hopes, and the fears, that humans cherish in respect of themselves, other people, animals and inanimate objects. The expectations one has with regard to personal development, career advancement and income are important indicators of future purchasing and investment behaviour, i.e. they have a direct behavioural relevance. When people can see difficult times ahead, for example, they start to save money – while at the same time they are more willing to borrow (Katona, 1960a, b).

Expectations that are associated with personal advantage or personal rewards are thereby imbued with a special desirability and worth. Attitudes are made up not only of opinions and views about a given object, but also value judgements. In this way a connection is established between attitudes and values; according to Kluckhohn (1967, p. 395), a value is 'an explicit or implicit concept of the desirable which is characteristic of an individual or group, and which influences the choice of behaviours and behavioural objectives'. Attitudes and hopeful, desirable expectations are thus closely bound up with the concept of values: both – attitudes of expectancy and values – differ in this respect only in that the latter are more general in their scope. Attitudes always relate to specific objects of opinion, and thus to specific behavioural alternatives, while values are much broader in their reference. Personal attitudes to various objects – and indeed to people, animals, the natural world, certain forms of behaviour – are essentially determined by these general values and the criteria by which they are measured.

This is not to say, of course, that we can satisfactorily explain human behaviour vis-à-vis concrete objects of opinion simply by knowing something about the general values to which a person subscribes. The fact that a person understands and accepts the values of Christianity, for example, does not necessarily mean that that person will behave helpfully in an accident situation (Schwarz, 1973). While it is clearly appealing to think that one might be able to predict a person's actual behaviour vis-à-vis various objects of opinion simply by identifying the few central values to which that person subscribes, research has shown that this is unfortunately not the case.

At both the theoretical and practical level, therefore, we must seek to establish a link between general values and ideals on the one hand, and specific situations and patterns of behaviour on the other. If a person's values constitute a schema of what is desirable to that person, i.e. what that person regards as necessary to the satisfaction of his needs, they also constitute the yardstick by which various alternative courses of action are measured. 'Sociability', for example, is always viewed as a positive value, an ideal. But the realization of that ideal may take many different forms, and the range of possibilities available to the individual is very largely determined by his personal ideals – a detailed analysis of which must form the first stage in any diagnosis. It therefore becomes important to know what alternative ways of attaining an objective, i.e. what alternative modes of action, are in fact available to a particular individual, given his previous life history. A person's values are manifested in his concrete wishes and desires, in his aspirations and standards, and only in *this* form do they have an influence on his behaviour.

What we might term the 'naive' fallacy in the study of attitudes and preconceptions has now been exploded. That is to say, we can no longer assume that just because a person expresses a certain opinion, has a certain attitude or holds a certain preconception, he will therefore behave in a corresponding manner. In short, it is 'naive' to infer actual behaviour in a specific situation from an expressed attitude to an object (Wicker, 1969). And because attitudes are no longer regarded as reliable predictors of behaviour, social psychologists have addressed themselves to two vital questions:

1. Under what personal, situational, social and cultural conditions do which attitudes, opinions, preconceptions and
   images have an effect on behaviour?
2. Which methodological conditions must be satisfied before we
   can hope to explain and predict specific behaviours and
   actions?

Since psychology relies very heavily on what people actually say
– and since the way in which a person perceives, evaluates and explains other people, animals, situations, events and objects constitutes his experiential environment, and hence the basis of all his
reactions – the spoken word remains, for social psychologists, the
essential starting point for an explanation of human behaviour.
What matters here are the specific criteria that need to be satisfied
before attitudes become useful indicators of actual behaviour.

A leading contributor to the ongoing critical discussion about
the relationship between attitudes and behaviour has been
Fishbein, who has formulated his findings in a number of theoretical models. In the first of these (Fishbein, 1967), behaviour – which
is always deduced from behavioural intentions – is dependent on
four factors:

(a) attitude to behaviour vis-à-vis a certain object;
(b) one's own belief in the rightness or otherwise of this behaviour
    ('subjective norm');
(c) how the intended behaviour will be judged by society, includ-
    ing reference groups or key reference persons ('social norm');
    and
(d) one's own willingness to behave in accordance with personal
    or social rules of conduct (norms).

In other words, behaviour reflects how far one is willing to flout
social rules of conduct in order to carry out one's personal
behavioural intentions. Fishbein emphasizes the importance of
'weighting' these four factors for individual subjects, but sees no
need to make an allowance for these variables in his methodology,
given that they can be measured empirically by regression
analyses.

In a second, shorter model (Ajzen and Fishbein, 1970), the only
essential requirements for the explanation of behavioural intentions are attitude to behaviour vis-à-vis a certain object and one's

own belief in the rightness of this behaviour. However, the results of the empirical analyses persuaded the authors to abandon this model in favour of the more comprehensive earlier version.

By 1972 Fishbein had developed a third model, based on a revised interpretation of the 'social norm', i.e. on the actual or supposed assessment of one's own behavioural intentions by others. Ryan and Bonfield (1975) have expressed the same idea in the form of an equation. In order to explain and predict a person's behavioural intentions with regard to a given object, we need to take account not only of his own attitude – appropriately weighted in terms of personal significance – but also of any relevant social reference persons, i.e. social norms.

Since then, Ajzen and Fishbein (1977) have proposed yet another model to explain the relationship between attitude and behaviour. Both are viewed as constituent parts of a single whole, with four aspects to consider in arriving at any explanation:

(a) a concrete behavioural act (e.g. the acquisition of a dog);
(b) the 'attractive' goal of this behaviour (e.g. the acquisition of a dog for one's own children);
(c) the situation in which the behaviour is to be enacted (e.g., keeping a dog in a rented city apartment); and
(d) the timing of the behavioural act (e.g. the forthcoming birthday of a child).

The basic premise of this model states that concrete behaviour can be more readily predicted the more closely the 'attitudinal unity' reflects the concrete 'behavioural unity', taking into account the above-mentioned situational and personal behavioural intentions. In other words, the two unities must correspond at the level of abstraction (Bergler, 1966). This model still awaits proper empirical verification, although, after analysing a number of studies to check the degree of correspondence between attitude and behavioural intention, Ajzen and Fishbein (1977) were able to establish a positive correlation between attitude and behaviour in those cases where attitudes were closely geared to a specifically defined form of behaviour. To cite a concrete example: if I wish to know whether a certain person is willing to become a bone marrow donor, it is not sufficient to know whether that person is willing to be an organ donor in any form, or indeed whether his general attitude to the donation of organs is a positive one. These questions are easily answered in the affirmative. What I need to ask about is his specific attitude to the donation of bone marrow, thus establishing a correspondence, in terms of specificity, between attitude to a certain form of behaviour and personal willingness to behave in that way.

Our own attempt to explain the relationship between man and dog is likewise based essentially on theories of attitude. But the 'ideal' expectancy values of the individual play a vital role in evaluating alternative behaviours, considered in relation to decision-making processes that are made up of value-oriented attitudes (the importance of certain needs) and attitudes that reflect the probability of attaining a given objective through various alternative courses of action. In fact all the Fishbein models, as they stand, must be rejected for the purposes of our inquiry, for reasons which are given below:

1. The close correlation between behavioural intention and concrete behaviour postulated by Fishbein appears highly questionable to us. The ultimate object of our inquiry, after all, is to explain and predict dog ownership and the conditions that conduce to dog ownership. This is not to deny that a statement of concrete intentions is a necessary stage in the generation of specific decisions: but this is by no means sufficient in itself (as indeed we know from our ordinary everyday experience). By making behavioural intention the sole predictor of behaviour, we only *appear* to resolve the theoretical difficulty of the relationship between attitude and behaviour.

   The low correlation between attitude and behaviour only serves to underline this difficulty, which is further aggravated by the fact that authors often over-interpret the coefficients of correlation yielded by their use of the Fishbein model and often attribute an excessive explanation value to the data (Ajzen and Fishbein, 1973; Ryan and Bonfield, 1975). Apart from one or two exceptions relating to choice of toothpaste brands (Wilson, Mathews and Harvey, 1975), the coefficients of correlation between behavioural intention and actual behaviour are no higher than .40 or .50. For marketing purposes, such findings are not sufficiently conclusive. In order to analyse the observed difference in the coefficient of correlation for different products and brands, we need to consider two aspects which seem to us to be especially relevant in any further theoretical discussion, i.e. the degree of complexity of a product (the difference between buying a tube of toothpaste and buying a new car, for example), and the degree of personal significance, or 'centrality', involved in a given purchasing decision. These two variables have undoubtedly played a significant part in determining the coefficient of correlation in past studies. From the findings available to us, it does rather appear that the explanation and prediction value of a Fishbein model decreases in inverse proportion to the complexity of the object under investigation.

2. The significance of the specific situation, in all its complexity, is virtually ignored (on the situational concept, see Petermann, 1985 and Pass, 1979). In his own model of the attitude–behaviour relationship, Sheth (1971, 1974) accords far greater importance to situational components – particularly in relation to the explanation and prediction of purchasing decisions – than (for example) Ajzen and Fishbein in the revised 1977 version of their model. The definition of a situation presents certain difficulties, as does the identification of the interactive processes that take place within a given situation, together with their consequences. Psychological research still has a long way to go in terms of refining the theory and application of situational and behavioural concepts. The significance of the situation and its various component parts have been analysed to some degree by market psychologists, notably in connection with the study of purchasing decisions. Here it can be shown that the influence of a shop assistant increases in inverse proportion to the confidence and competence of the customer faced (for example) with the purchase of outerwear or complicated electrical appliances. In other words, purchasing intentions expressed prior to the purchasing situation may be materially changed as a result of situational factors (see also Bergler, 1982).

It is clear, even from these examples, that further theoretical discussion of the relationship between attitude and behaviour will need to focus more closely on these components. As far as the subject of our present inquiry is concerned, it is undoubtedly fair to say that people differ from each other in terms of the extent to which they feel knowledgeable about dogs and/or keeping a dog – or indeed the extent to which they actually *are* competent in this regard. The same applies to persons of significance in one's own social environment, in so far as the degree of competence attributed to a given individual is a direct measure of that person's influence in any decision-making situation that might arise.

3. Attitude to behaviour vis-à-vis a certain object, as it is understood by Fishbein, fails to take account of the complexity, or multi-dimensionality, of the attitude systems that govern moti-

vation. Motivational psychology has already shown that human behaviour is always rooted in more or less complex motivational states (Thomae, 1983).

Independently of this, social psychologists have been able to demonstrate (Bergler, 1965, 1966) that 'attitude' – understood here not just as an affective response (De Fleur and Westie, 1963) – is not a one-dimensional phenomenon, but that attitudes towards animals (for example) incorporate many different components. The satisfactory explanation and prediction of concrete behaviour requires an approach that takes into account the multi-faceted complexity of an attitude system, together with its personal significance and connotations for the individual concerned. Only such an approach can yield a meaningful description of concrete motivational states in terms of behaviourally relevant attitudes. In other words, it is not only necessary to establish a correspondence between attitude and behaviour in terms of the level of abstraction or specificity: it is also vital to ensure that there is a correspondence between the object of an attitude and its configuration within the subjective and group-specific attitude system. And this must be duly reflected in the methods used to collect and analyse the data.

4. Fishbein's model neglects the personal weighting, or centrality, of an object of opinion. People express opinions on, and adopt subjective attitudes to, a wide range of objects, but this is not to say that they attach equal importance and relevance to them all. We approach different objects of opinion with varying degrees of interest and commitment. When a given object, experiential state, goal, desire or mode of behaviour seems particularly important to us, we tend to discuss it far more intensively – and therefore in a way that is far more behaviourally relevant – than opinion objects of little intrinsic interest. But in order to explain and predict concrete behaviour, it is also essential to discover what significance and what degree of ego involvement are associated with a given attitude object, such as a dog, and with the various cost and benefit factors of a dog, i.e. the various components of an attitude system that affects the decision-making process. Thus a certain individual or group of individuals may value a dog more highly for its role in preventive health care than as an object of affection to be stroked by its master. For other people, the priorities might be completely reversed. In short, we need a theory and a methodology that take into account the individually relative 'centrality' of the various components in an attitude system (see also studies in

the phenomenology of 'involvement and commitment' by Festinger, 1957; Brehm and Cohen, 1962).

5. Apart from one or two passing references, Fishbein also ignores the fact that desirable personal goals can be attained in a variety of different ways, i.e. that human behaviour is always essentially an individual process of choosing between alternatives on the basis of a more or less conscious weighing-up of desirable benefit factors and undesirable cost factors. Attitudes vis-à-vis a given object are always related in some way to attitudes vis-à-vis other, and often alternative, objects or behaviours. Thus the contemplated purchase of a dog may be a choice between a number of more or less conscious alternatives, of whose existence – and personal significance, or centrality – the research worker must be aware in order to maximize the predictive value of attitudes. The importance of such factors is particularly apparent in the context of purchasing decisions, while the problem of concurrent motives is a familiar one in the psychology of human personality (see Wicker, 1969; Gross and Niman, 1975).

Exchange theory

Social psychologists have also evolved conceptual models based on cost/benefit theories that have been developed in the course of research into economic decision making (games theory). The so-called 'exchange theory' of Thibaut and Kelly (1959) is primarily a theory of social behaviour, i.e. it attempts to explain and predict processes of social interaction between two individuals. In its more developed form it is also applied to the behaviour of fairly large groups – and indeed to the interaction between people and objects. In the present context, of course, we are concerned specifically with the interaction between humans and pets.

This theory views interpersonal, or social, behaviour as something which is determined by the balance of perceived advantages and disadvantages, or in other words, by the psychological cost and benefit factors involved: and these in turn are understood as a consequence of intended or actual behaviour. It is assumed that an individual only chooses a certain behaviour if he expects to gain some personal advantage thereby, or if this behaviour has previously resulted in a pleasurable outcome and therefore arouses the expectation of a reward. 'As a general principle, anything that makes interaction easier is regarded as a *reward* by the person for whom the interaction is thus facilitated, while anything that makes interaction more difficult is regarded as a *cost* by the person for whom it is thus complicated' (Bierhoff, 1973, p. 301).

Every form of need-fulfilment in the broadest sense, i.e. the attainment of personal goals and ideals, must be viewed in this sense as a reward, a benefit factor, a perceived positive behavioural consequence. In terms of the present inquiry, this means that the behaviour we term 'purchasing a dog' becomes more probable the more perceived positive consequences (and the fewer perceived negative consequences) are expected or remembered from previous experience of dog ownership. Behaviour is always circumscribed by specific situations and conditions and occurs in the context of various possible choices. In other words, the decision to purchase or not purchase a dog cannot be isolated from the question of how far a dog is capable of fully satisfying human needs – and whether there are alternative ways of satisfying those aims, desires and needs.

All such decision-making processes thus involve a subjective evaluation of the cost and benefit factors based on a subjective level of aspiration and the perceived behavioural alternatives available at a given point in time ('comparison level of alternatives'). Bierhoff (1973, 1974), who formalized and refined the exchange theory, has elucidated these two data, which are so vital to the theory. The term 'comparison level' refers to the mean value of all experiences (consequences) that one has had in comparable situations in the past, which now determines one's level of aspiration in situations currently arising. Put more concretely, this means that if one has achieved success in earlier performance situations, one will want to maintain or enhance one's standard of personal performance. If this has *not* been the case, the result will be a certain lowering of one's personal level of aspiration. In other words, what one sets out to achieve is not some absolute value, but a relative, biographical one, which is constantly changing and evolving. Applying this analysis, once again, to the subject of our present inquiry – the decision whether or not to purchase a dog – the theory would assume that in the course of his development a person arrives at a kind of 'ideal profile' of a dog, which thus constitutes his 'level of aspiration' as the standard and yardstick by which all dogs are measured.

To summarize the argument so far, the more the costs are outweighed by the benefits, and the more closely a specific dog approaches one's own ideal of what a dog should be, the more probable the acquisition of a dog becomes. Now we must consider the so-called 'comparison level of alternatives'. To acquire or not acquire a dog is not simply a matter of choosing between different breeds of dog, but of choosing between a dog and other possible behavioural alternatives, which may satisfy a certain basic human need in the individual equally well, or better, than the acquisition of a dog. Forced to choose between qualitatively different alternatives – such as a very attractive girlfriend who dislikes dogs, and a dog – a person will decide against the dog if the girlfriend occupies a place of central importance in his life, *even though* the dog might correspond to his personal image of the ideal dog. However, if we take the case of an old person living alone, who values dogs very highly and does not have any positive alternative means of communication and social contact, then the theory would lead us to expect that that person *would* acquire a dog.

Ultimately, the two comparison levels represent a further process of evaluating behavioural consequences, that is, any explanation of human behaviour depends to a large extent on the relationship between the actual or possible consequences of a behaviour and the available standards of comparison. Now in order to explain, and if possible predict, behaviour by relating an evaluation of the psychological costs and benefits to the various standards of comparison, exchange theory needs to draw on other theoretical models, such as the theories of cognitive dissonance, balance and attribution. Bierhoff (1973, p. 312) has pointed out that exchange theory only 'corresponds to reality . . . when other theories are invoked in its support'. If this is the case, then the theory itself needs to be reformulated. Exchange theory has made a valuable contribution to social psychological research in the area of interpersonal relationships, as an instrument for explaining how couples come to form close relationships, how social conflicts arise, etc. But it does not furnish an adequate basis for explaining and predicting human behaviour: its data, often defined with insufficient precision, are not sufficiently complete to satisfy the requirements of a theory.

Quite apart from this there is the problem of operationalization, i.e. translating theory into practical method (Harris, 1976). Thus while authors have repeatedly emphasized the complex structure of the two comparison levels, they have failed to develop a methodology that adequately reflects that complexity (Festinger, 1942). We readily acknowledge the key role played by exchange theory in stimulating the further development of an attitudinal–behavioural theory of decision making. Our inquiry therefore begins with a critical look at what exchange theory has to tell us about the relationship between attitudes and behaviour.

1. The ideal profile or standard (the expectations and aspirations that appear especially important when the cost and benefit factors are weighed up) is always geared to the specific opinion object, which in our case is dogs, their advantages and disadvantages, their reward and punishment value. No attempt is made, in preliminary studies, to clarify the specific importance to the individual of those human needs and values that a dog (or some other 'vector') might be able to satisfy in some degree. Instead, the ideal values are largely considered in the context of the object. This is a plausible approach, but it seems to us that one should be asking under what conditions the subject- or object-related level of aspiration, and under what conditions the general values underlying human behaviour – in terms of desirable life goals – should be used as the yardstick for evaluating the cost versus benefit factors. Where the objects at issue are products or services, the appropriate yardstick is undoubtedly the ideal profile of the product itself (which of course embraces both the product's suitability for its practical purpose and its ability to satisfy certain psychological needs). However, where we are dealing with human beings and animals, with interaction and communication, then the particular 'opinion object' in question is probably better seen in terms of its function as an instrument for the realization of personal ideals and values.

    Our own model, therefore, is based on the view that we should *begin* by establishing subjective hierarchies of need – discovering how important certain values, experiences, needs, desires and behaviours are to the individual. Only then, in the second phase of our study, do we turn our attention to dogs and their potential role in the attainment of these goals.

2. Psychological cost/benefit factors are of limited value in explaining and predicting concrete behaviour, even when such aspects as their personal significance (the extent to which they approximate to the ideal profile) and the individual's comparison level of the alternative behavioural possibilities at a particular point in time are taken fully into account. Human behaviour does not conform to some mechanistic economic model, whereby cost factors are simply subtracted from benefit factors to leave a 'balance remaining'. This is dramatically underlined by a finding that recurs frequently in studies on the motivation of human health behaviour (Bergler, 1984).

    Smokers and non-smokers alike are equally aware of the possible advantages and disadvantages of smoking, and both groups regard good health as a major priority. Yet the two groups adopt radically different patterns of behaviour. In order to explain such behaviour, we must look beyond the process of weighing benefits against costs. The 'cost/benefit' model merely tells us the degree of importance attached by the individual to the attainment of a certain benefit or the avoidance of certain costs. Such cost and benefit factors can have no real explanation value for human behaviour unless they in their turn are psychologically weighted. Therefore, in addition to the intrinsic personal significance of the various psychological benefit and cost factors, we have also taken into account the probability of their incidence in the eyes of the individual concerned. In other words, we have attempted to establish how far the individual thinks it likely in his particular case that a certain pattern of behaviour – such as cigarette smoking (Bergler, 1984), the use of body-care products (Bergler, 1986), the acquisition of a dog, etc. – will actually be followed by the desired benefit factors or possible cost factors. Exchange theory as such makes no provision for any influence of subjective probabilities on the evaluative process.

3. The results of psychological research into many different areas of human behaviour have clearly shown that while there may well be room to refine exchange theory still further, it is still necessary to adduce additional factors ('moderator variables') to explain and predict behaviour. Compared with traditional attitude–behaviour models, our own approach significantly enhances the explanation value of such models – particularly for complex decision-making processes – by incorporating certain aspects of advanced exchange theory. Even so, however, we still need to take into account other explanatory factors. In the case of purchasing decisions, for example, the actual purchasing situation – with all its attendant variables such as presentation of merchandise, quality and competence of sales personnel, etc. – also has a part to play.

   Similarly, the purchase of a dog by a family is not simply determined by one individual's evaluation of the relative costs and benefits, and his weighting of that evaluation in the light of certain standards and values. Instead it is usually based on discussion, controversy and compromise with the other members of the family, that is processes of social interaction, communication and group dynamics. The fact is that any theory based exclusively on exchange values, however modified and reformulated, is unlikely to furnish a satisfactory explanation of human behaviour vis-à-vis an object or subject. Subjective satisfaction with the level of correlation between attitude and behaviour, or with the 'explanation' of behaviour yielded by analysis of variance, is very common among research psychologists – and very understandable in human terms. But from a scientific point of view, and as a theory of human action, it is altogether unsatisfactory and naive. Nearly 25 years have passed since Karl Bühler published his book on the 'crisis in psychology': but unless research psychologists can solve these basic problems of theory and method, they must be prepared for continuing criticism of their discipline for the next 25 years as well. Our own view is that the problems *are* soluble, provided we can overcome a rigid adherence to established research models – and thereby inject a little much-needed creativity into the theoretical debate.

A theoretical model

Few would disagree that any explanation of everyday human behaviour and experience must be founded on a 'good' theory. The basic requirements of such a theory are that it should describe the complex state of affairs that it seeks to explain – e.g. the acquisition and ownership of a dog and its significance for human well-being – as simply, economically and elegantly as possible. In order to assemble a sufficient body of data and interpret them in a meaningful way, the manner of their collection must itself be directed by a clearly focused theory: only on the basis of such findings is it possible to develop and refine the theory itself. Individual aspects and findings all need to be integrated into a logical system of determining factors and interrelationships. When people speak of the 'practical' value of theories and models, we need to remember – and particularly in the case of psychological theories – that the limits of their validity must always be borne in mind, no less than the danger of over-simplifying reality, i.e. the particular behaviour which the theory is designed to explain. There is also a further danger here, in that the essentially *provisional* character of theories is not sufficiently recognized – which is why theories often prove resistant to new ideas and observations.

The various theoretical positions discussed above, together with their shortcomings, have prompted us to develop our own theoretical model, which is designed to explain the relationship between man and dog and to explain and predict the acquisition of a dog under specific psychological, economic and ecological conditions. We pointed out earlier that this model is based both on research into the correlation between attitude and behaviour and on exchange theory, with some attempt to combine the two. At the same time it takes account of additional influential factors (intervening variables) of a personal, social and situational nature. The elements, or constructs, that make up the model are shown in diagrammatic form in Fig. 7. In this model we have included a number of factors that we were not able to take into account in the present study. These are the result of extensive theoretical discussion and are based on findings that had been established previously. Principal among them is the methodological problem, thus far unresolved, of the psychological weighting of alternative behavioural options, i.e. how do we assess to what extent, and with what degree of probability, dog ownership is better able to satisfy basic human desires, goals and needs than other forms of behaviour? Or to put it another way: how do we establish the ranking of dog ownership within the 'comparison level of alternatives'? 'Social factors' are another element in our model that is still in need of further study.

The acquisition of a pet and one's relationship to it is undoubtedly influenced by the actual and anticipated reactions of other people in one's immediate social environment. What is ultimately at issue here is the degree of perceived social support for one's own desires and needs. This can work in a number of different ways:

(a) Family members, partners, friends and acquaintances may be credited with varying degrees of competence in the matter of dog ownership, so that their views are accorded varying weight in any discussion on the subject.

(b) The personal significance that one attaches to another person, i.e. the degree of positive dependence on that individual, determines the extent to which that person's view of pets (i.e. negative or positive) reinforces one's own estimate of the cost factors – and hence affects one's own decision-making behaviour.

(c) Even the anticipated likelihood of positive or negative reactions from social reference persons whom one particularly respects is a factor that has a very real influence on one's own decision-making processes.

(d) The tendency of psychologists to steer clear of 'interaction' (often for reasons of methodology), and the practical difficulties of carrying out the necessary research, mean that virtually no attempt has been made to 'profile' those other persons who help to determine a concrete behavioural act, i.e. studies tend

Fig. 7 Proposed theoretical model

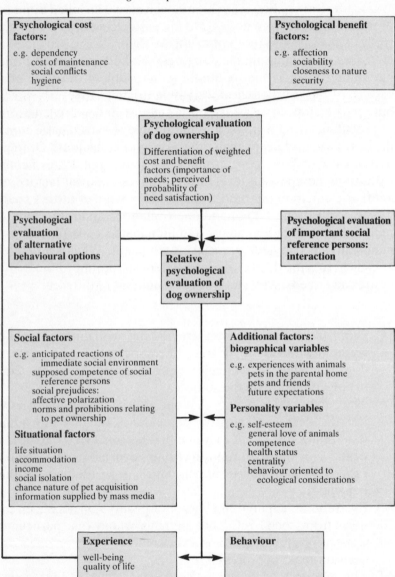

to confine themselves to a single individual (in this case, a dog owner or a non-owner). In other words, the anticipated or actual reactions of social reference persons who strongly influence a particular behaviour are *not* taken in to account. Ideally – and the proposed model makes provision for this (see Fig. 7) – we would want to ascertain the psychological weighting of important reference persons (partners, children, friends, acquaintances) and diagnose their influence on the relative psychological weighting or evaluation.

Besides these variables, a number of other factors influencing human behaviour and experience have also been taken into account in the present study. Undoubtedly there is scope for refining the model still further. This applies both to so-called biographical variables (the relationship between humans and pets in the parental home, with particular reference to the children's responsibility for pet care), and to a range of social and situational factors (e.g. anticipated reactions of key persons in the immediate social environment and their supposed competence in the matter of dog ownership; norms and prohibitions relating to pet ownership, e.g. in rented apartment buildings; information supplied by mass media, etc.). The findings of the present study are based on the theoretical model outlined above. They represent an attempt to explain and predict the relationship between man and dog – and ultimately, human behaviour and experience – in terms of the following factors.

Psychological cost and benefit factors associated with dog ownership (independent variables)

The psychological cost and benefit factors associated with dog ownership, weighted according to primacy of human needs and values and the perceived probability of their attainment, are the essential basic data for explaining behavioural motivation. Taken together, these factors add up to a general psychological evaluation of dog ownership, in which the balance of pros and cons is largely determined by individual motivation.

Additional factors (intervening variables)

The present study also takes into account the following factors, identified on the basis of previous research into the relationship between humans and pets:

Current life situation

Here we are concerned to establish the outward circumstances of a person's life – we need to know such basic personal particulars as age, income, occupation and family status, together with details of living accommodation (size of house or apartment, location of same, garden facilities, etc.). At the same time it is important to ascertain the person's general life habits (typical patterns for normal weekdays, weekends and vacations) in order to establish whether dog owners and non-owners have their own characteristic 'life-styles'. The essential issue here is whether and to what extent a person's life-style is influenced by a dog, and under what conditions such influence is desirable, acceptable, or not acceptable to the individual concerned. In short, a person's life situation and life-style must be viewed as additional incentives or barriers to dog ownership.

Experiences with pets in the course of one's life (biographical variables)

If it is possible to categorize people according to whether they grew up with animals in the parental home or not, then it seems reasonable to assume that such qualitatively different conditions of development might also encourage different attitudes to animals in general and to dogs in particular. It was therefore necessary to establish to what extent the individual had had encounters and experiences with animals in general (i.e. any pleasant or unpleasant incidents associated with animals) and pets in particular (including responsibility for pets in the parental home) at any stage of his biographical development.

Future expectations

A person's willingness to acquire a dog is undoubtedly influenced to some extent by thoughts about the future, i.e. one's personal psychological evaluation of dog ownership is partly determined by the vision one has of one's own future development in terms of goals and aspirations. A person who loves animals and evaluates dog ownership very positively may nevertheless decide not to acquire a dog (or replace a dog that has died) if his own health status or life expectations are such that it would not be in the dog's own best interests.

Personality characteristics

Repeated attempts have been made in the published scientific literature to explain dog ownership – and by the same token, non-ownership – with reference to general personality characteristics (see
Chapter 3). In our own psychological pilot study the following
characteristics were studied: self-esteem; extraversion/introver-
sion/neuroticism.

- 'Self-esteem' refers to the extent of positive attitudes towards
  one's own person (Argyle, 1972). It is the combined product of
  self-perception and interpretation of one's social environment,
  and it is of central importance for the quality and intensity of
  individual behaviour.
- Extraversion/introversion and neuroticism/emotionality are
  two dimensions of personality which have often been invoked to
  explain behavioural differences. There is also a certain amount
  of empirical evidence to suggest that a person's general well-
  being – and perhaps his perceived quality of life as well – are significantly influenced by these personality traits (Costa and
  McCrae, 1980). However, the unsatisfactory results yielded by
  our pilot study persuaded us to omit any consideration of these
  personality factors from our representative main study.

Social prejudices: affective polarization

It is clearly the case that some people hold entrenched opinions, or
prejudices, on the subject of dog owners and non-owners. The
more qualitatively different these social prejudices are, the greater
is the social distance between owners and non-owners. This can
lead to a hostile attitude (affective polarization) which is not without influence on the possible – and in personal terms, perhaps,
desirable – acquisition of a dog. It is therefore necessary to establish the self-image of dog owners and non-owners respectively,
together with the image that each group has of the other. At the
same time it would seem important to ascertain how dog owners
imagine they are perceived and evaluated by non-owners – and
vice versa.

Behaviour and experience (dependent variables)

The theoretical model we have developed purports to describe,
explain and predict the behaviour and experience of persons who
differ from each other in terms of the criterion 'dog ownership'.

Three categories of behaviour are distinguished here: current dog owners, non-owners of dogs, and owners of other pet species (e.g. rabbits, budgerigars, cats).

The experiential dimension is explored in terms of subjects' general satisfaction with their own lives and a specific sense of well-being associated with dog ownership. 'Well-being' and 'satisfaction' are always defined as subjective variables. It was therefore necessary to arrive at a separate determination of the meaning and interpretation of these two quantities.

Working hypotheses

The following working hypotheses were formulated on the twofold basis of the theoretical model developed for this study and the results of our systematic survey of the published scientific literature:

General hypotheses

Hypothesis 1: The acquisition of a dog is more probable, the more likely it is that central subjective needs, desires and values will be satisfied thereby – and the more unlikely it is that the acquisition of a dog will be associated with inconvenience, personal detriment or conflicts.

Hypothesis 2: Satisfaction with one's own life and a personal sense of well-being are positively correlated with the quality of one's psychological evaluation of dog ownership.

Hypothesis 3: Dogs tend to be evaluated more positively by dog owners than by owners of other pet species; the lowest positive scores and the highest negative scores are found among persons who do not keep pets of any kind.

Special hypotheses

With an increase in positive scores on psychological evaluation, the acquisition of a dog becomes more likely:

● the less social stimulation a person is exposed to, i.e. the more that person is socially isolated;
● the more directly involved with pets a person has been during childhood, with particular reference to responsibility for feeding and general pet care;

- the more personally significant, or 'central', a dog is for an individual's well-being;
- the less attractive alternative behavioural options are;
- the more a dog is taken for granted as a natural part of one's expectations and plans for the future;
- the less positive and stable one's own feelings of social assurance and self-esteem;
- the more one's own development and memories have been marked by positive experiences with animals, and the fewer negative experiences one has had;
- the more favourable the conditions affecting one's life situation (living conditions, income, rent agreements, etc.);
- the fewer negative attitudes and prejudices are anticipated, or actually present, in key social reference groups or individuals;
- the more one knows about the psychological and therapeutic significance of a dog.

Structure of study and sampling techniques

The complexity of the phenomena under investigation, the significant lacunae in previous research work (as demonstrated above) and the absence of methods suitable for use by empirical social researchers in interviewing a cross-section of the population obliged us to adopt a two-stage approach.

Psychological model study

The purpose of this study was to offer a differentiated analysis of the motivational states that conduce to the purchase of a dog, and to identify the barriers that stand in the way of such a purchase. At the same time, the model study was designed to clarify the nature and variability of additional factors, together with possible correlations between dog ownership and individual quality of life. In terms of methodology this was an exploratory pilot study, i.e. the questions were all open-ended, with no preselected list of alternative answers. This was the only reliable way of assembling a truly representative item pool (Bergler, 1975) that would reflect the full spectrum of possible experiences and attitudes, cost and benefit factors, motivational states, biographical and situational factors, social prejudices, etc. Only then was it possible to formulate further working hypotheses on the basis of our theoretical model – and of course the subjects' replies at this stage furnished us with the necessary raw data for constructing attitude scales and questionnaires. The principal areas explored by the pilot study were as follows:

- Personal desires and values relating to everyday life, leisure and other people.
- Analysis of the concepts 'quality of life' and 'well-being'.
- Psychological context and associations evoked by the subject of dogs.
- Past experiences with animals.
- Biographical aspects of the relationship to dogs and other pets.
- Perceived advantages and disadvantages of dog ownership.
- Images of dog owners and non-owners: friend/foe stereotypes.
- Personal significance of dog ownership.
- Personality characteristics such as self-esteem, extraversion, neuroticism.

A total of 80 subjects were interviewed for an average period of two hours each. The sample consisted of 40 dog owners and 40 non-owners (of the latter, 20 had never owned a dog, while 20 had owned a dog previously).

The subjects were further categorized as follows:

- Current dog owners living alone.
- Current dog owners living with a partner.
- Current dog owners living with a partner and children.
- Previous dog owners living alone.
- Previous dog owners living with a partner.
- Previous dog owners living with a partner and children.
- Persons who had never owned a dog, living alone.
- Persons who had never owned a dog, living with a partner.
- Persons who had never owned a dog, living with a partner and children.

*Main study**

The questionnaire developed on the basis of the psychological model study was administered to a population sample comprising 930 people. The final sample was arrived at via a two-stage process. First, a representative random sample of 500 people was selected

*The fieldwork and basic tabulation of the raw data were carried out by the MAFO Institute in Schwalbach, using a questionnaire devised by the author. My thanks are due to Dr Bruckert and his staff for all their invaluable assistance.

on the basis of demographic characteristics, then interviewed. In terms of ownership/non-ownership of pets, this sample was structured as follows:

280 people with no pets in the household.
 92 people with a dog in the household.
128 people with other pets (e.g. cats, budgerigars) in the household.

Secondly, as we wished to assemble sufficient data to formulate plausible hypotheses about all three groups, the two last-named groups were augmented by the addition of further subjects, selected on the same demographically representative basis. Our final findings and interpretation were thus based on a total sample made up as follows:

280 people with no pets in the household.
345 people with a dog in the household.
305 people with other pets in the household.

The essential demographic characteristics of this sample survey are shown in Table 8.

Table 8 Demographic data

	Respondents with dog in household n = 345	Respondents with other pets in household n = 305 (%)	Respondents with no pets in household n = 280
Sex			
Male	47	46	47
Female	53	54	53
Age			
14–19 years	12	19	4
20–29 years	13	14	15
30–39 years	18	18	17
40–49 years	22	22	19
50–59 years	19	14	15
60–69 years	10	7	15
70 years and older	6	6	15

Table 8 *contd.*

	Respondents with dog in household n = 345	Respondents with other pets in household n = 305 (%)	Respondents with no pets in household n = 280
Family status			
Single	22	30	17
Married	63	56	64
Widowed/divorced/ separated	12	12	17
None stated	3	2	2
No. of people in household			
1 person	9	13	23
2 people	30	26	34
3 people	27	26	20
4 people	22	22	20
5 or more people	12	13	3
No. of children and adolescents in household			
Children below the age of 6	8	11	15
Children aged between 6 and 14	22	22	17
Adolescents aged between 14 and 18	25	28	10
Educational qualifications or last school attended			
Primary school	66	59	68

Secondary school, no
    school-leaving exam./
    several yrs at business or
    technical school
	24	28	21

School-leaving exam.	6	5	5
College/university	3	7	5
None stated	1	1	1

Table 8 *contd.*

	Respondents with dog in household n = 345	Respondents with other pets in household n = 305 (%)	Respondents with no pets in household n = 280
Occupational status			
Working full time	51	49	46
Not working	49	51	54
Type of work			
Owners or managers of large companies, company directors	–	–	–
Self-employed businessmen, owners of small firms, self-employed skilled tradesmen	2	2	3
Liberal professions	1	3	1
Senior clerical grades	1	3	2
Other clerical grades	17	22	16
Senior officials	1	–	1
Officials, other grades	3	3	5
Skilled workers, skilled tradesmen employed by others	16	8	13
Other wage earners	6	5	6
Self-employed farmers	2	1	1
Agricultural labourers	–	–	–
None stated	2	2	3
Pensioners, retired persons, unemployed	49	51	49
Social status (interviewer's assessment)			
Upper class/upper middle class	31	27	29
Lower middle class	59	66	60
Working class	10	7	11

Table 8 *contd.*

	Respondents with dog in household n = 345	Respondents with other pets in household n = 305 (%)	Respondents with no pets in household n = 280
Combined household income (net)*			
Less than DM 999	4	2	4
DM 1000–1499	9	9	16
DM 1500–1999	12	15	15
DM 2000–2499	17	20	13
DM 2500–2999	18	15	20
DM 3000 or more	30	26	24
None stated	10	13	8
Size of locality (no. of residents)			
Up to 1999	12	4	5
2000–19 000	35	32	28
20 000–49 999	17	20	14
50 000–99 000	9	10	16
100 000 or more	27	34	37

*The amounts have been expressed in DM as in the original survey. At the time of English publication the exchange rate was DM 3.03 = £1.00.

Table 9 Current ownership of pets other than dogs

	Respondents with dog in household n = 345	Respondents with other pets in household n = 305 (%)
Cat	10	38
Budgerigar	11	41
Canary	3	13
Other cage birds excluding pigeons	4	6
Other pets, e.g. hamster, guinea pig, tropical fish	8	19
No other pets	64	–

Table 9 indicates which types of animal were owned by the 305 persons with pets other than dogs in their household.

Following the basic study carried out in 1983, two further investigations were undertaken in 1984. One was a psychological follow-up study on the subject of 'dogs and the elderly', while the other was a representative survey of the population based on a sample of 4000 people. Here again, the main objective was to analyse the process of psychological evaluation in order to arrive at valid conclusions about certain social groups (defined by age, sex, etc.) with regard to dog ownership, non-ownership of dogs and ownership of other pet species.

Although the sheer volume of the material defies comprehensive presentation, the results of these two studies are cited selectively wherever they serve to reinforce or illuminate the findings of the basic study.

7   Results of the study

The psychological foundations of dog ownership

Dogs and the quality of life: benefit factors

Our survey of the research literature had already revealed a multiplicity of positive experiential states associated with dog ownership. At the same time it was apparent that the German-speaking scientific community still has a great deal of work to do in this area. Therefore, before proceeding to the development of quantitative methods, it was necessary to analyse the various qualitative dimensions of the man–dog relationship, in order to have a better understanding of the psychological environment of dog owners and non-owners respectively. It is worth pointing out, however, that even some persons who do not own a dog associate very positive sentiments and ideas, amounting to a sense of personal well-being, with a dog. Equally, it can be shown that under certain circumstances dog ownership may entail certain restrictions and inconveniences, in addition to the psychological benefits that it can bring. A decision for or against the acquisition of a dog is always the product of a more or less conscious process of evaluation and personal 'weighting' of those (often highly emotional) factors that help to enhance personal quality of life, and those rather more rational factors that tend to detract from it.

The quality of the relationship between humans and dogs – and hence the contribution a dog can make to personal well-being – are systematically analysed below on the basis of our findings in the qualitative pilot study. The experimental aspects are further illuminated with reference to typical replies from respondents, before a final interpretation is offered. The statements derived from these replies then form a basis for developing the methodology used in the representative study. The resulting attitude scales yielded data that were then subjected to further statistical analysis. Using the techniques of factor analysis, we were once again concerned to isolate and identify the basic conditioning factors of the man–dog relationship.

The dog as social stimulus

We humans view dogs essentially as social beings, whose behaviour is perceived and evaluated in interaction with our own behaviour. Dogs are a focus of attention for humans, forcing us to be sociable, to 'join in' and engage in play. They impart joy and satisfaction, they banish feelings of loneliness, they provide 'someone to talk to', and they stimulate certain kinds of activity. In short, the dog is a creature with which one can develop a stable, positive emotional relationship. This basic, generalized function as 'social stimulus' can be further analysed into a number of specific components.

The dog as companion

The development of a permanent and lasting relationship between pets and humans leads people to speak in terms of 'friendship' or 'comradeship'. A dog has the ability to embody, to 'act out', as it were, a range of emotional needs whose satisfaction is vital to human existence – such as the need for understanding, loyalty, support in times of crisis, gratitude and sympathy:

' . . . my dog is a real companion for me; to me a dog means having a friend; a dog is a lifelong companion; a dog is a friend on life's journey; a dog will go through fire and water for its master's sake . . . '

' . . . dogs are very loyal; most dogs are very faithful creatures; a trusting animal; a dog requites the love you give it three times over; dogs are very loyal creatures – in fact they are almost more reliable than humans . . . '

' . . . life is full of hassles, but my dog is a friend I can always rely on; my dog adds another dimension to my life; gives me a great deal of pleasure; is a lot of fun; a source of pleasure and enjoyment . . . '

' . . . helps me not to feel lonely; you don't feel so alone; you don't feel so lonely with another living creature around; because I live alone a dog is especially important to me as company; it's like acquiring a new member of the family; a dog is good company . . . '

' . . . I talk to my dog a lot; I talk to my dog about all kinds of things that interest me; somebody to talk to . . . '

' . . . watching the dog is like a real breath of nature; it's always fascinating to watch him; it's an aesthetic delight to watch him . . . '

' . . . the dog understands me and my problems; nobody knows me better than he does; I get the feeling that he really understands me . . . '

' . . . you can really play well with him; he loves it when you romp around with him; play with him a lot; he's a great playmate . . . '

' . . . the dog is my cuddly pet; dogs give you a tremendous amount of affection; I like him and he likes me; someone to hug and cuddle . . . '

' . . . a dog's gratitude is a real source of joy; it warms your heart to see how grateful he is . . . '

The dog as fulfilment of emotional needs

Although this potential role was mentioned above, we may now add one further aspect, namely the ability of a dog to impart a sense of emotional and psychological security. The stabilization of one's own self-esteem depends in no small measure on the realization that one can elicit warmth and affection from another human being – or a dog. Some people take this to the point of believing that their pet actually 'understands' them.

The dog as a leisure activity

Dogs are an established part of people's routine and life-style. This applies particularly to their leisure time, the use of which is determined in part by the demands of their pets:

' . . . it's important for me that I do a lot of walking, and the dog is an enormous help in that way; the time I spend with the dog is mainly taken up with long walks and "getting back to nature"; to me the dog means going for walks and feeling healthy . . . '

'... the dog takes my mind off my problems; is a distraction; if I've been having trouble with people he helps me to forget all about it; he takes my mind off the day-to-day grind ...'

'... with a dog you've got to go out in the fresh air every day; it helps me overcome my laziness and gets me out of the house ...'

'... anyone who has a dog gets "exercised" by the animal; I get out at least twice a day with the dog; the dog needs to be walked, it's good for your health, you don't get out of shape because you get plenty of exercise every day ...'

In this way a dog influences the way a person spends his spare time. This is seen by and large as a positive stimulus, a form of relaxation, a distraction from the cares of everyday life. The dog *forces* its owner to do something in his spare time, and thereby helps him to get more enjoyment out of life.

The dog as an instrument of preventive health care

This aspect of dog ownership is primarily associated with the use of leisure time that a dog dictates. People regard exercise as healthy, and they are pleased that the dog forces them to get out in the fresh air regularly, regardless of the weather. In short, dogs help their owners to stay fit and healthy.

The dog as partner in education and upbringing

While dog owners themselves are often very emphatic about the positive 'educational' influence of their dogs on their own life-style, the educational significance for their children is not usually taken so seriously. It is as if people believe *in theory* that a dog has great educational potential for a child, but doubt *in practice* whether a child is really prepared to take on the responsibilities associated with looking after a dog.

'... a dog requires discipline; the dog forces you to adopt a regular routine; you have to be organized, because the dog needs regular care and attention; it forces you to get up at the same time every day – after all, you have a responsibility; you can't just drift along; you have to maintain a certain daily rhythm; I need something to make me get my act together; the dog gives a definite shape to my day . . . '

' . . . a playmate for our children; such a wonderful playmate, all children ought to have one; a dog helps children when they're growing up, the children learn to take on responsibility; looking after the dog teaches children what it means to have specific duties; the children learn to relate to animals by growing up with the dog; the children learn to assume responsibility on a regular basis – it keeps them out of mischief; is an ideal playmate for our daughter; children should get used to being around animals from an early age . . . '

Parents ascribe a valuable role to dogs in the education of their children (and this is a point that really ought to be emphasized more strongly) because their own association with an animal has led them to see a potential for teaching socially desirable behaviour. They believe that by learning to understand a dog, a child will have a better chance of understanding other people and identifying with their situation. There is a further aspect here, in that dogs are also seen in the role of protectors. If a child is accompanied on his walks by a dog, then he is undoubtedly able to explore his environment more easily and readily, without feelings of fear or insecurity. In other words, a dog can also 'teach' a child personal security, self-assurance and self-confidence, thereby making an important contribution to his personality development.

The dog as challenge and responsibility

Dog owners undoubtedly see their pets as a positive challenge, as creatures for whom one gladly and willingly assumes a responsibility and an obligation, whom one is privileged to care for:

' . . . the dog gives me someone to care for; you've got a job to do; you have a useful occupation; the dog gives you something useful to do, it creates a kind of relationship, someone I can look after and care for . . .'

It is worth pointing out here that elderly people are particularly prone to the belief that they are not needed any more, that they have no responsibilities and are therefore superfluous. When there are no longer any demands being made on them they easily fall victim to resignation and depression, and they start to neglect themselves.

In this situation a dog can help simply by virtue of the fact that he 'takes a person in hand', forcing him to adopt a regular daily routine and a more active pattern of behaviour. One is forced to perform certain tasks, to assume responsibility for a dependent (in the positive sense) living creature. Such experiences of mutual dependency are a necessary part of meaningful human existence: the prognosis for the future development of persons on whom no demands are placed is *not* encouraging (Walster, 1979).

The dog as protector

Respondents repeatedly emphasized the feeling of security they owed to the vigilance of a dog, i.e. its 'deterrent potential':

> '. . . the dog gives me protection; dogs protect you; my dog is kept as a guard dog; the dog is there to guard the house; my last dog once bit a drunk who tried to grab hold of me . . .'

> '. . . there's no fear of being attacked; he protects you; you feel safer in the house with the dog there; he warns you when somebody's coming; as a woman I feel safer at night with a dog; I'm less frightened if somebody comes to the door when I'm alone; is a good watch-dog; he barks if he hears something . . .'

All these replies refer in the first instance to physical protection against human aggression. However, the feeling of physical safety is closely associated in its turn with feelings of mental security and well-being.

The dog as a creature without moods

One of the major psychological benefits of dog ownership is that the animal's affection is seen as a behavioural constant, i.e. not determined by situational factors:

> '. . . my dog is always friendly to me, I can depend on that; he's a loyal soul who is totally devoted to me; is pleased to see me, regardless of the mood I'm in; the dog is always friendly . . .'

In other words, the dog displays a constant – and virtually unshakeable – emotional attachment to its master. It is precisely this capacity for unchanging affection towards humans which makes dogs eminently suitable for use in therapy. One simply cannot imagine a dog *not* being pleased when one comes home: it is only humans who are moody and influenced in the display of their affections by situational factors.

The dog as an embodiment of success

The dog is also seen as a creature that rewards its human master. This is especially apparent in the way a dog is often seen as a 'willing pupil', whose progress and achievements are felt to be a direct reflection of one's own progress and achievements. In other words, the dog 'rewards' its human master in the form of successful achievement:

> '. . . the dog obeys me instantly; he's very willing to learn, you can teach him a lot; dogs are the most intelligent of all pets; he's eager to learn; you can teach him very easily; he's wonderful to train; he's very well trained, we go to lots of contests; I feel I've really achieved something worthwhile when he does what I tell him; it's really interesting to train him and teach him . . .'

The dog as mediator of social contacts

A dog can also be a means of establishing desirable social contacts. It is easy to get into conversation with other people about a dog, especially if they are dog owners themselves. The dog as a topic of conversation thus serves as a basis for contact between individuals:

> '. . . it's easy to get talking to other people about the dog; we've made a lot of new friends through the dog club; we've made a whole new circle of friends, thanks to our dog; dog owners are all alike in some ways, the dog creates a bond between individuals; I often talk to people about my dog; through the dog I've got to know some very nice people, other dog owners, and now we often go walking together . . .'

The dog as prestige object

This refers to the fact that the socially acknowledged attractiveness of a dog, particularly a pedigree dog, sheds a kind of 'reflected glory' on its owner, i.e. enhances his own social standing:

'. . . when you own a beautiful dog you've got something you can show people with pride; many dog owners regard their dog as a kind of prize exhibit; some people use their dogs to show off; it's a status symbol . . .'

In short, it is possible to enhance one's personal prestige, either consciously or unconsciously, by means of a dog. Social recognition, reinforcement of one's self-esteem and an increase in one's own social attractiveness are directly associated here with dog ownership.

In the first instance, therefore, the psychological study underlines the many possible contributions a dog can make to personal well-being and quality of life. The positive benefits of dog ownership may be summarized as follows: less stress, more general contentment, a greater sense of inner harmony, enhanced sociability, reinforcement of one's self-confidence and the feeling of having a task to perform – which in turn lays the foundations for experiences of personal success and fulfilment. At the same time a dog can make people more open to their immediate social environment, enrich their experience of nature, keep them fit and healthy, be a friend and companion to them, assist them to make new friends, provide a sense of physical and mental security and enhance their personal prestige, i.e. their own social attractiveness.

Obstacles to dog ownership: cost factors

In considering the contribution a dog can make to personal quality of life and analysing the statements on that theme, we also need to inquire about the possible detrimental effects of dog ownership on the quality of life. This in itself, of course, tells us nothing about the actual or anticipated extent to which a dog can negatively influence a person's well-being. At this point we shall simply catalogue all the possible negative experiences associated with a dog that were mentioned by the subjects in our study.

The dog as a financial cost factor

The financial cost of dog ownership is a rational argument that becomes critical only if the owner is experiencing genuine economic hardship. The difficulties of maintaining an adequate standard of living are cited even when the emotional arguments in favour of a dog carry far more weight. In the final analysis, people do not begrudge the money they spend on their dog:

'. . . the biggest expenses are his food and the dog licence; I have to spend a lot of money on my poodle; the costs are sometimes pretty high – for example, every three months he has to be professionally groomed; I often get annoyed about the cost of the dog licence; a dog occasionally gets ill and has to be taken to the vet – and that doesn't come cheap . . .'

The dog in the home

This cost factor comes into play when one wishes (or is forced) to move into a smaller house or apartment, at which point there may be a problem about finding enough space for a dog. Naturally this depends in part on the size, habits and needs of the dog in question. If these needs are not satisfied, the result is likely to be conflict (in the broadest sense of the term) between humans and pets – conflict which is felt to be damaging to the animal itself, and therefore detrimental to its owner's quality of life:

'. . . we could only get a dog if we moved into a larger house; our house is too small for a dog; there wouldn't be enough room in this house; it's difficult when the dog can't get outside and run around; I couldn't think of getting a dog unless I had a house with a garden; our rental agreement specifically states that we're not allowed to keep any pets; we would have to move . . .'

A number of respondents mentioned that their rental agreements forbid them to keep a dog. In the absence of comparable alternative accommodation free from such restrictions, even persons with a positive psychological evaluation of dog ownership will not acquire a dog.

The dog as time factor

This refers to the time which has to be spent in looking after a dog. While this is certainly not an ongoing problem for dog owners, there are always situations where there is not enough time for a dog, and where a dog may therefore be seen as a relative nuisance:

'. . . dogs take a lot of looking after; you have to devote a lot of time to a dog; a dog immediately means more work; you have to spend time caring for a dog . . .'

'. . . a dog makes work; there's a lot of extra work involved; you have to spend a lot of time looking after him; you've always got to be looking after him, keeping an eye on him; you can't just stick him in the corner every time he becomes a nuisance; a dog demands a fair amount of your time; you're saddled with him the whole time; it takes up a lot of your time, and sometimes it's a real nuisance that you can't just open the door and let him out, instead of having to go "walkies" with him; it takes up a lot of time, but I don't really mind that . . .'

So while on the one hand a dog may encourage a person to adopt a more structured daily routine and engage in healthy activities, he may on the other hand be seen as a burden sometimes, precisely because the owners is tied to a regular round of feeding, grooming, going out for walks, etc.

The dog and hygiene

Here again the arguments and reservations put forward by the respondents were primarily of a rational nature.

'. . . dogs always make me think of all the dog muck in the parks; dogs make a mess; to me a dog means mess; dog's piss; the dog makes a lot of mess; when you own a dog your car is permanently dirty . . .'

'. . . the dog gets into the bed and leaves hairs everywhere – I don't like that; the dog sometimes climbs onto the bed and makes it dirty . . .'

The hygiene problems associated with dog ownership may be divided into three categories:

1. Lower standards of cleanliness in the home. The need to accept a lower standard of cleanliness and tidiness in one's own home is a point that is often raised in discussions, not least by dog owners themselves. The point is significant, because for many people less cleanliness in the home means a lower standard of domestic life – less 'comfort' in the broadest sense – which in turn impairs their sense of well-being.

2. Hygiene in public places. This particular issue is the subject of frequent public debate. It becomes personally significant and painful when it gives rise to conflict between individuals, i.e. whenever a dog owner feels threatened by other people because of his dog's behaviour, has to apologize for that behaviour, and is unable to appease objections with the argument that he 'has paid his dog licence fee'. Here is a classic situation in which a non dog owner feels his quality of life threatened by another person's dog.

3. Risk of transmitting diseases. The risk of a dog owner contracting a disease from his dog is slight, provided that the dog is well cared for and common-sense hygiene precautions are carried out. However, recent cases of serious illness, sometimes leading to blindness have been shown to be caused by the *toxicana canis* bacterium, transmitted to children when they come in contact with dog faeces, especially in parks where there is a high concentration.

Suggestions for dealing with this problem have included the provision of dog-exclusion zones in parks where children can play in an uncontaminated environment. Dogs should also be frequently wormed.

The dog as conflict factor

In discussing the various aspects of the hygiene problem above, we saw how other people can feel disturbed or even threatened by the behaviour of a dog, i.e. how a dog can be a cause of interpersonal anxieties, fears and conflicts. The kind of negative experience that can arise in connection with a dog is best illustrated in the respondents' own words:

'. . . all that barking drives me crazy; dogs mean one thing to me: noise!; next door's dog always barks at the postman; dogs make a lot of noise when they bark. . .'

'. . . you have to be careful with dogs, they often bite; a dog once bit me on the hand; only a week ago an Alsatian bit me on the knee. He was very friendly at first, and I was stroking him, when all of a sudden he bit me – I have no idea why . . .'

'. . . the dog created problems with my boyfriend, the dog was jealous and always barked at him; the dog places itself between my girlfriend and me . . .'

'. . . the dog can sometimes be disobedient and bite somebody, and then you're responsible as the owner of the animal; our last dog was very unreliable, he wouldn't think twice about biting somebody . . .'

'. . . we're always having trouble with the neighbours, they can't stand dogs; as soon as the dog barks, the neighbours get uptight; the neighbours get annoyed if they hear him howling in the house when we're out; problems with the landlord . . .'

While dog owners and non-owners undoubtedly differ with respect to the various aspects listed here, their meaning and psychological evaluation, one general point emerges: easy as it is for the individual to imagine his own contact with dogs as an entirely positive experience, it is quite clear that dogs *can* constitute a risk factor in interpersonal relations. Possible areas of conflict may be defined as follows:

- Problems with neighbours and landlords: excessive noise, lack of hygiene.
- Difficulties with one's partner (and possibly the children too).
- Other people potentially at risk from the unpredictable or aggressive behaviour of a dog.

It is reasonable to assume that in all cases where the risk of such problems is high, there exists a very real obstacle to dog ownership.

The dog as a restriction on freedom of movement

The possibility of unwelcome restrictions on one's own freedom of movement is something that dog owners themselves have to face in certain situations:

'. . . you can't just take off in the holiday period, you have to get somebody to look after the dog; there are always problems with the dog when we want to go on holiday; holiday times are always the most difficult; because of the dog we have to restrict our holiday plans somewhat . . .'

'. . . in a way you're tied to the dog; being tied; you have to be there all the time; it's very hard to do anything on the spur of the moment, I always have to think of the dog; the dog is a real tie, there are some places where you simply can't take a dog; when I go out anywhere in the evenings I can't stay late because he can't be left on his own too long; since I've had the dog it's not so easy for me to go out to the cinema . . .'

'. . . even when I can't really spare the time I have to be there for the dog; you always have to be around, even when you don't feel like it; you have to arrange your whole life around the dog; it's hard, having to take him out at a certain time every day, whatever the weather; you have to take him "walkies", even in the pouring rain; you have to plan your day around the dog; I can't just sit back and take it easy when I feel like it, I have to think about the dog; I get less chance to lie in in the mornings because he always wants to go out early . . .'

Owning a dog can mean, therefore, that one feels restricted in one's personal freedom of movement and one's leisure opportunities. One feels hemmed in – even to the point where one decides to get rid of the dog, or not to acquire a dog in the first place. And if a person *does* feel that his mobility and leisure opportunities are severely curtailed, he will automatically see this as highly detrimental to his quality of life. Under such circumstances the dog detracts from, rather than enhancing, the person's sense of well-being.

The dog as 'dependent'

A pet is always viewed as a creature that is dependent on human beings and the care and attention they give. Older people living alone, in particular, fear that illness or death will prevent them from looking after their pet. This can detract from the pleasure afforded by a dog. The extent to which this may be associated with negative feelings of worry and anxiety is illustrated by the following replies:

'. . . I'm afraid that one day my health won't be up to looking after him; problems if I fall ill and can't attend to his needs; I couldn't keep the dog if I fell seriously ill and found I couldn't look after him . . .'

'. . . if I got a dog he would be certain to outlive me, and I don't know who would look after him when I'm gone; I can't do that, I would worry too much; I'm too old for a dog, what would happen to him when I die, who would look after him . . .'

Summary

Summarizing our qualitative findings in respect of all the many factors associated with dog ownership that can influence personal quality of life positively or negatively, we arrive at the 'for and against' profile shown in Table 10.

Table 10   Positive and negative factors associated with dog ownership

Positive factors

- Social stimulation
- Companionship
- Relaxation
- Leisure activity
- Preventive health care
- Friendship/comradeship
- Protection
- Emotional attachment and security
- Regular, structured routine
- Positive challenge and responsibility
- Help with bringing up children
- Understanding and sympathy from the dog
- Rewarding sense of achievement
- Aid to social contacts
- Prestige

Negative factors

- Restricted freedom
- Financial cost
- Expenditure of time
- Hygiene
- Problems with neighbours, etc.
- Family difficulties
- Possible risk to other people
- Problems with dog in case of owner's illness or death

In the next section we shall seek to establish which positive factors – and indeed which negative factors – dog owners are aware of, and what significance is attached to them in personal experience and decision-making behaviour.

8 Positive psychological evaluation of dog ownership

Well-being and quality of life

Before inquiring more closely into the expected and probable contribution made by a dog to the fulfilment of personal needs and aspirations, we need to establish what exactly people understand by well-being and quality of life. We would then expect to find a direct correlation between the extent to which those specific needs are fulfilled, and a person's general experience of well-being and quality of life.

'Well-being' and 'quality of life' are terms that are constantly bandied about these days by politicians, scientists and laymen alike. As we know from studies in the social psychology of language, the widespread use of a term does not mean that everybody uses it in exactly the same sense: on the contrary, wider currency encourages a multiplicity of meanings. 'Well-being' undoubtedly belongs in this category of terms with 'elastic' meanings.

The difficulties of defining this term satisfactorily are also apparent from a study of the relevant psychological literature (Andrews and Withey, 1976; Pervin and Smith, 1986; George, 1979). From these works one may conclude in the broadest sense that the experience of well-being – a sensation of physical and mental relaxation and harmony – occurs when an individual's need structures, level of aspiration and desired self-image are answered and satisfied by correspondingly attractive objects in the immediate environment and their interpretation by the individual. The critical factor is the individual's subjective life space, i.e. his objective circumstances as such matter less than the way he perceives and evaluates them.

Applying this analysis to dog ownership, what matters is not what a dog *is*, but what he *means* to his owner (or potential owner). Any psychology of well-being must therefore begin by establishing which areas of life – in the sense of goals and aspirations – are important to a person (such areas typically include health, friends, work, pets, etc.), and what criteria are appropriate in evaluating them, i.e. what qualities are desirable in those areas (typical criteria might be 'enjoyment', 'comfort', 'variety', 'independence', etc.). Andrews and Withey (1976), for example, have designed and tested a model that covers 123 such areas of life.

If we look at the psychology of everyday life and ordinary linguistic usage, we find that the two terms 'well-being' and 'quality of life' overlap a good deal in terms of meanings, ideas, associations and evaluations. Thus both have to do with satisfaction, being happy, and feeling free from stress. Other important areas of life associated with 'quality of life' and 'well-being' are interpersonal relations, relationships with friends and acquaintances, family, marital relationship and health status.

Other things which significantly affect 'quality of life' and 'well-being' are a person's living conditions, private activities, cultural pursuits, going to parties, eating out in restaurants and holiday travel. A positive commitment to one's work is also an important factor, of course.

We may proceed on the assumption, therefore, that 'quality of life' and 'well-being' are very similar in their range of meanings, even though there may be certain differences of nuance. 'Quality of life' is perhaps more readily associated with affluence, freedom from financial care and a decent standard of living – although it may also refer to more abstract ideals, such as a clean and healthy environment or peace and quiet. On balance, 'quality of life' tends to be more abstract in its range of meanings, and is not without a certain ideological component.

'Well-being', on the other hand, is something more tangible and concrete, such as having a hot bath, listening to music, having a lie-in or drinking a fine wine. It can also refer to emotional feelings of happiness, such as being in love, going for a walk in the country-side, owning a dog, passing an examination, relaxing by the fire, etc. A sense of inner harmony, having somebody one can confide in, social recognition and success, not being lonely – these are some of the feelings we associate with 'well-being'. All in all, therefore, 'well-being' tends to connote experience of a concrete, situational nature. The range of meanings covered by the two terms, as revealed in our psychological pilot study, may be summarized in tabular form, using the spontaneous ideas and associations volunteered by the respondents (see Table 11).

Taking our cue from the scientific literature on the subject, we might also define 'well-being' and 'quality of life' as that condition in which human needs, values, desires, goals and aspirations find their fulfilment. That the dog has a very real contribution to make – at least for dog owners – to quality of life and well-being is readily

Table 11   Range of meanings covered by the terms 'well-being' and 'quality of life'

Inner harmony
Warmth, affection, security

Trust in another person
Pursuing one's hobbies

Listening to music
Fine wines, good food

Love, being in love
Success, social recognition

Wedding, marriage
Weekend

Enjoying the countryside
Owning a dog

A job that I enjoy
Husband/wife and family

Fine weather
Sociability

Security
Peace and quiet

Health, fitness
Friends

Vacations
A nice house

Being at peace with oneself
Absence of stress

Concerts, theatre, films, etc.
Receiving sympathy and consolation

Affluence

---

apparent from the spontaneous replies recorded in the course of our psychological pilot study:

'. . . for me, my dog is an integral part of quality of life; I felt especially good when I first acquired a dog; I always feel especially good when I take my dog for a walk; the pleasure the animal gives me; the enjoyment he gives me; he's a constant joy to me; he adds something to my life; on the whole I have a very good time with the dog; he's a joy to me; he's become very dear to me; I would miss him if he wasn't there, he's like one of the family, we all love him; having someone around me that I like; having another living creature around me; it gives me an emotional point of contact when I'm alone; he's become my best friend; the feeling of having a pal; we have each other, he knows me and I know him; I can go for walks with him; because of the exercise; because having the dog is good for my heart; the exercise is good for my health; I never felt so unwell as I did the time my dog was run over; a few weeks ago my dog ran away, and I felt really ill, thinking something awful had happened to him; I've had the dog two years, and we have a lot of fun together; the dog gives me a great deal of enjoyment; it's nice to see so many dogs around; for me the dog is someone who understands my feelings; I've always had dogs around me, ever since I was a child; I've always loved dogs . . .'

Clearly dog owners, for their part, have no difficulty at all in establishing a direct correlation between personal well-being, quality of life, and the presence of a dog. As will be shown in more detail below, the majority of dog owners regard their dog as an established part of their system of social relations. He is a 'member of the group', and in the case of persons living alone he may constitute a kind of social group – a source of sympathy, happiness, friendship, companionship, joy, amusement, understanding, relaxation, etc. These are all states of feeling and experience that may be associated with one's own dog.

Personal desires, values and needs

Before inquiring into the reasons or motives for dog ownership, we must first of all establish, independently of the fact of dog ownership, which states of feeling and experience, i.e. which values and aspirations, conduce in what degree to quality of life and well-being for a given individual. In identifying these basic components of quality of life, it is important to ascertain whether a dog is able to influence significantly the realization of certain positive aspirations, thus leaving aside for the moment any consideration of the role and significance of a dog, we need to know (for example) whether people from households where there are dogs or other pets attach particular value to not being alone, being in the company of other people, caring for somebody or lavishing affection on them – or whether they particularly value their own health, having a fixed daily routine, etc.

Having thus established which individual or group of individuals harbours which hopes or fears – and with what degree of intensity – we then need to ascertain more specifically how far these people believe that the goals and aspirations they cherish for their lives can be attained with the aid of a dog. How likely does it appear to them that the attainment of these goals will be facilitated – or alternatively hindered – by dog ownership? It is also necessary to establish, very specifically, whether a dog owner *not only* attaches particular importance to not being alone or lonely, but whether he *also* believes that this desire for sociability and togetherness can be satisfied in a particularly positive way by a dog. Or, to choose another example of a more negative kind: do people who value their independence highly, who like to carry on without responsibilities and come and go as they please, believe that a dog would impose significant restrictions on the personal freedom they enjoy?

The psychological model study began by answering the question: what goals and values associated with individual quality of life may relate directly or indirectly to the psychology of dog ownership? In other words, we began by charting the possible spectrum of psychological benefit and cost factors (representative item pool), together with their psychological significance and function (instrumentality) for human experience and behaviour. The respondents' replies yielded a mass of raw material, which was then condensed into a series of succinct statements covering the entire range of possible benefit and cost factors. Subjects interviewed in the representative study were then invited to comment on these statements, indicating the degree of personal significance they attached to them, and the replies received were subjected to further statistical analysis. In particular we were concerned to clarify two questions:

1. What are the basic and non-interdependent benefit and cost factors associated with dog ownership?
2. Do the various subject groups actually use different factors to evaluate dog ownership, or do they simply differ in terms of the significance they attach to those factors?

First, the findings were analysed to establish the degree of personal significance attached to the predetermined aspirations and values by the individual. It may be generally observed at this point that dog owners, respondents with other pets in the household and respondents with no pets exhibited only very minor differences with regard to the degree of personal significance attached to the various aspirations and needs. Indeed, significant variations do not occur precisely because the present study is based throughout on the strict criterion of so-called 'practical significance'(see explanatory note in the Appendix).

Hypothetical questions about whether (for example) dog owners attach more importance to having a regular daily routine, or whether they value their health more highly than the other subject groups, must be answered in the negative.

The principal central values, needs and goals that were found to shape subjects' lives may be summarized as follows:

- Personal health status.
- Humanity/sympathy.
- Cleanliness and hygiene.
- Understanding and sympathy: having other people who can understand one's problems.
- A good romantic/marital relationship; love – affection.
- Enjoyment of life: leisure activities.
- Attractiveness of the environment.
- Social stimulation: communication.
- Social recognition.
- Enjoyment of nature: leisure activities.
- Physical exercise, leading an active life: a positive awareness of the body.
- Friendship and companionship.
- Good relations with the neighbours.
- The experience of personal freedom of action.

These are all qualities, states of feeling and experiences which are valued particularly highly by the respondents, and which they wish to attain if at all possible. In terms of qualitative volume, the social environment – or the 'communicative virtues' (Schmidtchen, 1984; Bergler, 1985) – clearly ranks as an item of outstanding importance.

We may therefore proceed on the assumption that these goals and values are more or less equally important for dog owners and non-owners alike.

Using the statistical technique of factor analysis (Überla, 1977), the large number of aspirations listed were further processed. Aspirations that are psychologically interrelated for a given individual – i.e. they are all expressions of the same underlying need – are grouped together as non-interdependent benefit factors. This procedure was carried out separately for each of the three subject groups (dog owners, owners of other pets, non pet owners), as well as for the entire combined sample. A further distinction was drawn between persons who, after evaluating all the cost and benefit factors of dog ownership, came to positive and negative conclusions respectively, irrespective of whether they owned a dog, another type of pet or no pet at all.

The first significant finding to be noted is that all three subject groups exhibit a very similar overall pattern with regard to the values and aspirations that determine individual quality of life and well-being. In Table 12 below the pattern for the combined total sample is presented in such a way that each factor is characterized by those specific aspirations and needs which ultimately define that factor's substance and content. The reader is also referred to the earlier summary of verbatim statements (see above, Chapter 7) on the various experiences and aspirations which together make up the field of personal *desiderata*.

Table 12   Factors which determine the quality of human life

Results of factor analysis: combined total sample
Analysed variance: 65.2%

Factor I:	*Sociability, social stimulation, communication*
	(.63) . . . that I have someone around me
	(.70) . . . that I have a companion, a friend
	(.72) . . . that I have someone I can talk to
	(.64) . . . that I have someone I can care for
	(.51) . . . that no harm comes to other people because of me
	(.61) . . . that somebody understands me and my problems
Factor II:	*Preventive health care*
	(.79) . . . that I often get out into the fresh air
	(.71) . . . that I get regular exercise
	(.70) . . . that I can get back to nature
Factor III:	*Enjoyment of life: distraction and recognition*
	(.75) . . . that other people acknowledge and respect me
	(.68) . . . that I have beautiful things around me
	(.53) . . . that I get to know other people
	(.51) . . . that I have a distraction from the normal everyday routine

Factor IV: *Safety and protection*
          (.66) . . . that I have someone I can teach something to
          (.61) . . . that I have somebody to protect me
          (.54) . . . that I don't have to move house
          (.54) . . . that I don't have to put up with a lot of noise

Factor V: *Independence, mobility*
          (.78) . . . that I can go where I choose for my holidays
          (.68) . . . that I have no ties which means that I can do as I
                  please

Factor VI: *Order and control over the environment*
          (.71) . . . that I have an established daily routine
          (.65) . . . that my flat/house is clean

Factor VII: *Love and sympathy*
          (.75) . . . that I have someone to play with
          (.67) . . . that I have someone to cuddle

Factor VIII: *Health and hygiene*
          (.76) . . . that I am in good health
          (.53) . . . that I have a fresh, clean bed

Factor IX: *Social independence and relief*
          (.84) . . . that there's nobody who's dependent on me, if I
                  should ever fall ill
          (.80) . . . that I don't leave somebody behind who's
                  dependent on me when I die

Factor X: *Marital relationship and children*
          (.76) . . . that my children are not put at risk
          (.73) . . . that I have some help with bringing up the children
          (.46) . . . that I have a good relationship with my marital
                  partner

Factor XI: *Frugality*
          (.76) . . . that my living costs are fairly reasonable

---

N.B. The figures in brackets are so-called 'loading values'. The loading value is a measure of the degree of correlation between a given item and a given factor. For example, in the case of the statement (or item) 'that I have a companion, a friend', there is a correlation of .70 with Factor I ('Sociability, social stimulation, communication'). The factor loading value can range from +1 (very high positive correlation), 0 (no correlation) and −1 (high negative correlation). Generally speaking, the items used to define the factors are confined to those with a loading value greater than .50.

We have already stated that the differences in factor structure between the various subject groups were only minimal. Such minor qualitative differences as did emerge between dog owners, owners of other pets and non-owners are briefly indicated below.

In the case of dog owners, for example, the ideals of a structured daily routine, order, cleanliness and frugality, together with the desire for well-regulated interpersonal relations, constitute a single non-divisible factor – which is not the case with the other two subject groups. From this it may be inferred that dog owners as a group regard a highly controlled and orderly environment (in the broadest sense) as a fairly important goal in their lives.

For owners of other pets, however, the desire for a structured daily routine and a house that is clean and tidy is independent of the desire to live in a pleasing and ecologically agreeable environment. Also, their relationship with their marital partner is qualitatively different from the one they have towards their children. The two factors are independent: children are invested with a separate value of their own, while the marital partner is placed in a wider context of interpersonal communication and sociability.

In the case of respondents who have no pets at all, it is apparent that health values are closely bound up with general mental well-being, enjoyment of life and friendship. A further difference also emerges, in so far as the desire for safety and protection is not automatically associated with the desire for mutual loving affection and sympathy, but is a separate factor in itself.

The significance of a dog for personal quality of life

It has already been shown that individuals differ very little or not at all in terms of the value they place on the component aspirations of quality of life, whereas their concrete behaviour may exhibit very considerable differences. For example, smokers and non-smokers alike attach great importance to good health, yet smokers differ from non-smokers in that they think it less likely that smoking will damage their health. But there is another variable at work here. Even where people differ very little or not at all in terms of basic aspirations and values, they may nevertheless adopt different techniques or 'instruments' to attain their goals. As the old adage reminds us all roads lead to Rome.

Thus, in order to explain and predict human behaviour and experience, it is not enough simply to draw up a catalogue of ideals and aspirations. What matters is to ascertain with what degree of subjective (i.e. perceived) probability certain specific aspirations and goals are attainable, for a given individual, through a certain specific form of behaviour or behavioural alternatives. To the extent that people differ as individuals, pets are also perceived, evaluated, liked or disliked in very different ways. By the same

token, a dog makes a uniquely individual contribution to the fulfilment of central needs – and hence to the experience of well-being
and quality of life.

We therefore need to look at the levels of probability with which
people believe (a) that a dog will help to fulfil certain specific aspirations judged by them to be of central importance, i.e. the advantages of dog ownership or benefit factors, or (b) that a dog will lead
to a relative deterioration in their quality of life, i.e. the disadvantages of dog ownership or cost factors.

We shall begin by looking at the 'advantages' of dog ownership,
as they were formulated by the various subject groups. Table 13
juxtaposes personal significance scores for general aspirations with
ratings indicating the level of probability with which the various
subject groups believe that a dog can help them satisfy personally
significant psychological needs. It is readily apparent, even from a
cursory glance, that there are a number of highly significant differences between dog owners as a group and those who own no
pets. In other words, the degree to which a dog contributes to personal well-being and quality of life is different for different people.

Statistical analysis of the differences between the various subject
groups shows that those who currently own a dog believe strongly
that their pet is a trusted and stimulating companion, ever-present
and ever-sympathetic. At the same time he distracts them from the
less attractive aspects of everyday life, and generally enhances his
owner's sense of well-being and enjoyment of life.

In the case of the other two subject groups, a dog's role in the
fulfilment of central personal aspirations is not so closely tied to the
communication function, but even here none of the findings is
totally at odds with those for dog owners. The only difference is
one of degree, i.e. a dog is thought to further the fulfilment of these
needs *to a lesser extent*. And in fact, when it comes to the protective
function of a dog and its potential role in preventive health care
(structured daily routine, exercise, contact with nature), all subject
groups are of the same opinion.

The most significant general point to emerge here is that
attitudes to dogs are not polarized in the way they are, for example,
in respect of alcohol consumption or cigarette smoking. The
number of people who conceive a generalized emotional aversion
to dogs is very small.

Table 14 shows the results of factor analysis performed on the
rating scale scores given in Table 13. If we look separately at the
three subject groups in terms of how the perceived benefits of dog
ownership are structured, we find the following factors occurring in

Table 13 Personal significance and perceived likelihood of possible advantages of dog ownership (mean values)

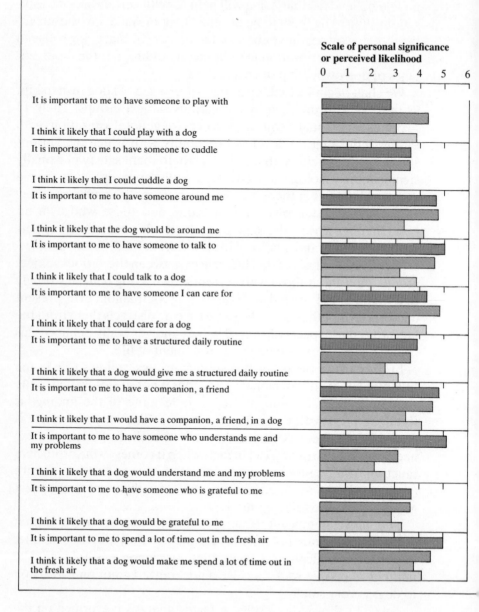

Scale of personal significance or perceived likelihood

0 1 2 3 4 5 6

It is important to me to have someone to play with

I think it likely that I could play with a dog

It is important to me to have someone to cuddle

I think it likely that I could cuddle a dog

It is important to me to have someone around me

I think it likely that the dog would be around me

It is important to me to have someone to talk to

I think it likely that I could talk to a dog

It is important to me to have someone I can care for

I think it likely that I could care for a dog

It is important to me to have a structured daily routine

I think it likely that a dog would give me a structured daily routine

It is important to me to have a companion, a friend

I think it likely that I would have a companion, a friend, in a dog

It is important to me to have someone who understands me and my problems

I think it likely that a dog would understand me and my problems

It is important to me to have someone who is grateful to me

I think it likely that a dog would be grateful to me

It is important to me to spend a lot of time out in the fresh air

I think it likely that a dog would make me spend a lot of time out in the fresh air

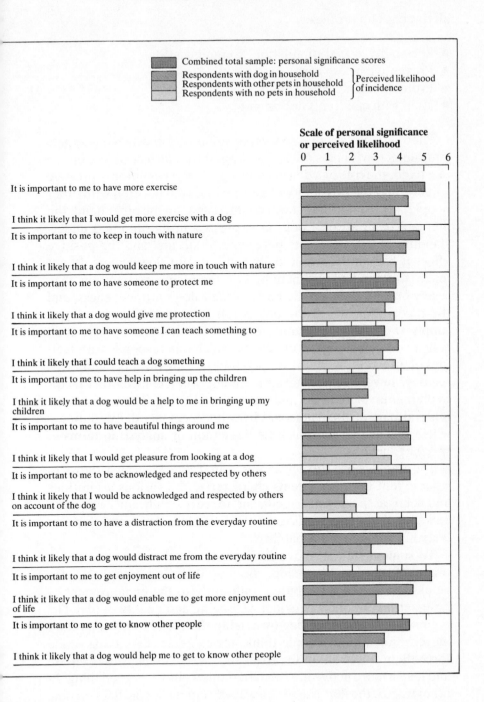

all three group profiles:

- Sociability, social stimulation, communication.
- Preventive health care.
- Protection and achievement.
- Help with children's upbringing.

There are certain differences, in so far as subjects with no pets and subjects with pets other than dogs distinguish between, on the one hand, the role of a dog in securing social recognition – 'prestige value' – and the possibility of getting into conversation with other people, i.e. establishing social contact, and, on the other hand, the 'human' qualities of a dog, as expressed in its supposed understanding of its master, its perceived 'gratitude' and the positive effect it has on the whole daily routine. But dog owners do not make this kind of distinction. For them, the recognition they receive from others on the basis of their dog's attractiveness, and the recognition which the dog is felt to accord its 'master', are simply two sides of the same coin. Those who have no pets at all concur in seeing dogs as objects to which one responds with feelings of affection, warmth and playful joy. Dog owners themselves see dogs in very general terms as an important contributory factor to their enjoyment of life and sense of well-being. Their pets are an integral part of their personal lives and personal daily routine – which means that there is little discussion or analysis in terms of *specific* functions.

The findings are further analysed in Table 15, which shows to what extent the respondents characterize the various aspirations and needs as 'personally significant' to 'very significant', while also believing that these needs can be satisfied by a dog with a 'high' to 'very high degree of probability'.

To summarize the above findings: the further removed one is oneself from dog ownership, the less likely it seems that a dog would be able to contribute significantly to the enhancement or safeguarding of one's personal well-being and quality of life. The arguments in favour of dog ownership then tend to be of a rather more rational kind. People think, for example, that a dog would force them to get out in the fresh air, take some physical exercise and lead a more active life – and that this would be a good thing. In other words, the dog is seen as a way of helping people to overcome their natural laziness in the interests of better health.

As for the other desires and aspirations to which people attach a high priority in their personal hierarchy of needs, a dog has only a

Table 14   A dog's contribution to quality of life (benefit factors):

Results of factor analysis: combined total sample
Analysed variance: 88.3%

Factor I: *Sociability, social stimulation, communication*
(.81) . . . that the dog would be around me
(.77) . . . that I could talk to a dog
(.77) . . . that I could care for a dog
(.62) . . . that I would get pleasure from looking at a dog
(.62) . . . that I could play with a dog
(.60) . . . that I would have a companion or friend in a dog

Factor II: *Preventive health care*
(.88) . . . that I would get more exercise with a dog
(.84) . . . that a dog would make me spend a lot of time out
in the fresh air
(.75) . . . that a dog would keep me more in touch with nature

Factor III: *Protection and achievement*
(.86) . . . that a dog would give me protection
(.61) . . . that I could teach a dog something

Factor IV: *Enjoyment of life*
(.76) . . . that a dog would distract me from the monotony of
everyday routine
(.65) . . . that a dog would enable me to get more enjoyment
out of life

Factor V: *Understanding and gratitude*
(.77) . . . that a dog would be grateful to me
(.68) . . . that a dog would understand me and my problems

Factor VI: *Emotional attachment: love and sympathy*
(.78) . . . that I could cuddle a dog

Factor VII: *Help with children's upbringing*
(.94) . . . that a dog would be a help to me in bringing up
my children

Factor VIII: *Prestige*
(.84) . . . that I would be acknowledged and respected by
others on account of my dog

Factor IX: *Mediation of interpersonal contacts (social catalyst)*
(.85) . . . that a dog would help me to get to know other
people

Factor X: *Structured daily routine*
(.62) . . . that a dog would give me a structured daily routine

(see note after Table 12)

Table 15 Psychological aspirations and needs

	Personal significance Total combined sample (n = 930)	Perceived likelihood of attainment through dog ownership (%)		
		Respondents with dog in household (n = 345)	Respondents with other pets in household (n = 305)	Respondents with no pets in household (n = 280)
Taking on a satisfying task, obligation, responsibility: active life-style enhancement or stabilization of self-esteem	72	85	62	55
Social stimulation: avoiding feelings of loneliness and boredom	80	84	59	51
Source of friendship, companionship	86	81	60	52
Experience of sociability, happiness and enjoyment of life: the dog as playmate	44	76	54	42
Preventive health care: a means to more exercise and contact with nature: freedom from stress	98	71	61	60

routine: feelings of variety, well-being and contentment: positive attitude to life	85	70	43	35
Source of sympathy and affection	60	63	33	29
Sense of achievement as a teacher: positive behavioural response and obedience from the dog	55	62	56	45
Source of protection and security	63	61	53	49
Experiences of gratitude and understanding	59	59	36	37
Experiencing a partner who is dependent, reliable and sensitive to one's own feelings	90	46	27	25
Guarantee of a regular daily routine	64	53	34	32
Encouragement and mediation of social contacts: the dog as social catalyst	73	52	35	25
Help with children's upbringing development of social skills and a sense of responsibility	32	36	21	20
Winning recognition and respect (prestige) from others	77	29	20	14

Table 16 Personal significance and perceived likelihood of possible disadvantages of dog ownership (mean values)

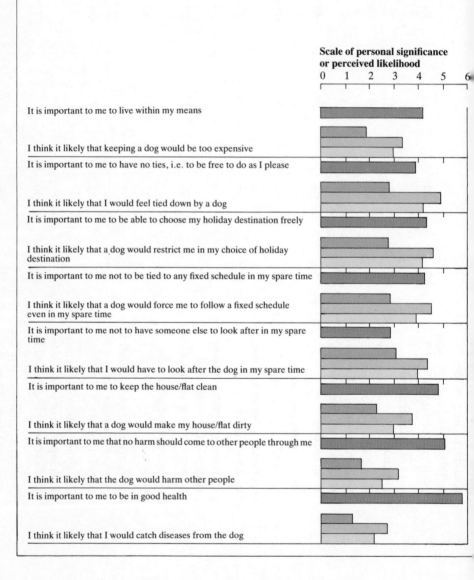

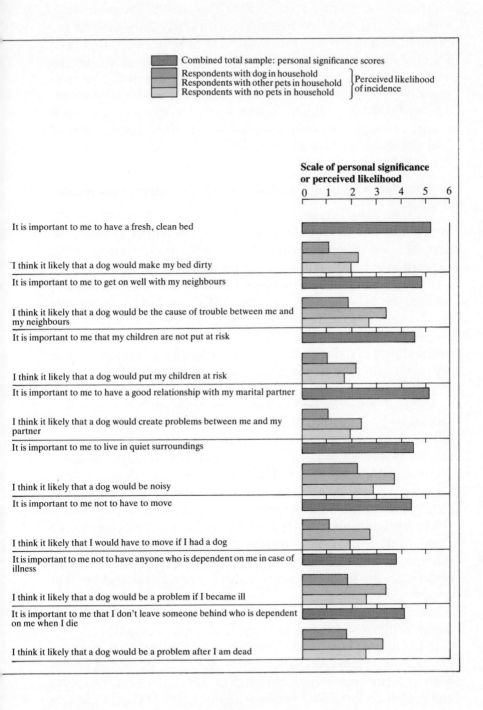

Combined total sample: personal significance scores
Respondents with dog in household
Respondents with other pets in household } Perceived likelihood of incidence
Respondents with no pets in household

Scale of personal significance or perceived likelihood

0   1   2   3   4   5   6

It is important to me to have a fresh, clean bed

I think it likely that a dog would make my bed dirty

It is important to me to get on well with my neighbours

I think it likely that a dog would be the cause of trouble between me and my neighbours

It is important to me that my children are not put at risk

I think it likely that a dog would put my children at risk

It is important to me to have a good relationship with my marital partner

I think it likely that a dog would create problems between me and my partner

It is important to me to live in quiet surroundings

I think it likely that a dog would be noisy

It is important to me not to have to move

I think it likely that I would have to move if I had a dog

It is important to me not to have anyone who is dependent on me in case of illness

I think it likely that a dog would be a problem if I became ill

It is important to me that I don't leave someone behind who is dependent on me when I die

I think it likely that a dog would be a problem after I am dead limited contribution to make to their attainment. The probability scores given in the table (mean values) clearly show that the acquisition of a dog is seldom accorded serious consideration. The essential motivation for the acquisition of a dog is lacking, for the simple reason that people cannot imagine dog ownership being in any way relevant to their own well-being. A largely rational consideration of the 'rational' advantages of dog ownership leads neither to emotional acceptance nor to a positive state of mutual dependency between 'man and dog'.

Perceived probability of a dog's negative impact on personal quality of life

In reaching any kind of decision, people are bound to weigh the desirable advantages against the possible disadvantages. The acquisition of a dog – and the many positive experiences associated with dog ownership – likewise involves certain relative disadvantages. However, the perceived likelihood of these possible disadvantages actually occurring is relatively low among dog owners (as compared with non pet owners). By the same token, it can be shown that dog owners have no difficulty in coming to terms with – and thereby neutralizing – such relative disadvantages as they do perceive.

We shall therefore be looking below at the so-called 'cost factors' of dog ownership. More specifically, we shall examine how likely it seems to the various subject groups that possible disadvantages of dog ownership will actually occur in their particular case.

Any weighting of these findings (in terms of 'explaining' motivation) is only possible when the significance scores for possible 'cost factors' are compared with their perceived likelihood of incidence. Since the significance scores for all three subject groups were the same, Table 16 has been compiled on the basis of a single set of significance scores for the combined total sample. These are compared with the separate group scores for perceived likelihood of possible disadvantages.

The differences between dog owners and the remaining subjects are immediately apparent and statistically well attested.

In the case of dog owners, there is a clear discrepancy between the personal significance of certain needs and the perceived probability of occurrence of subjective cost factors, i.e. the central values and goals associated with personal quality of life are not negatively affected in any lasting way by dog ownership. The only potential area of conflict and negative experience is that of personal inde-

pendence. Other, theoretically possible cost factors of dog ownership – such as financial cost, hygiene problems, problems with the
neighbours, family difficulties, danger to other people, problems
with the dog in case of own illness, etc. – are seen by dog owners as
non-applicable in their particular case, i.e. their well-being is in no
way affected thereby.

The ability of dog owners to come to terms relatively easily with
the possible disadvantages of dog ownership is illustrated by the
following arguments, put forward in response to some of these
objections.

- The expenditure of time required by a dog is equated with time
  well spent on oneself or one's family
- Restrictions on one's freedom of movement arise only occasionally: it is not a permanent problem.
- The financial expenditure incurred for a dog is insignificant
  when considered in relation to the psychological/emotional and
  therapeutic benefits.
- Keeping a dog is in no way incompatible with a high standard of
  hygiene. Dogs are no dirtier than humans.
- Problems with the neighbours can be avoided by proper training
  of the dog and good communication with the neighbours.
- A dog has to bark sometimes, if he is to carry out his protective
  function effectively.
- Even if its owner is ill, a dog will always find people to look after
  it.

Clearly, then, the possible disadvantages of dog ownership are
considered by dog owners to be insignificant in relation to the
advantages, while the vast majority of dog owners have no difficulty in adjusting to specific cost factors. But if we look at those
subjects who have no pets (and they differ as a group only insignifi-
cantly from subjects with other pets in the household – see Table
16), we find a widespread anticipation of emotionally disturbing
experiences. This applies particularly to the feeling of dependency,
the restricted freedom of movement and the expenditure of time
that dog ownership is expected to entail. There is also a relatively
high perceived probability of problems occurring in the case of
one's own illness, while certain difficulties are anticipated with
neighbours and other residents. Here, it is felt, a dog would be a
cause of conflict rather than an aid to personal well-being. Finally,
non-owners fear problems with hygiene, both in terms of cleanliness in the home and the risk of personal infection.

It is interesting to note that even non-owners do not anticipate *all* the possible disadvantages of dog ownership to the same extent. There *are* areas which are not perceived as problematic – or only very marginally so. But this does not alter the basic fact that the

Table 17   Dog ownership and possible negative influences on quality of life (cost factors)

Results of factor analysis: combined total sample
Analysed variance: 87.4%

Factor I: *Hygiene and risks to health*
            (.81) . . . that a dog would make my bed dirty
            (.75) . . . that I would catch diseases from the dog
            (.69) . . . that the dog would harm other people
            (.48) . . . that a dog would make my house/flat dirty

Factor II: *Restricted mobility: lack of freedom*
            (.88) . . . that a dog would restrict me in my choice of holiday destination
            (.84) . . . that I would feel tied by a dog
            (.64) . . . that a dog would force me to follow a fixed schedule even in my spare time

Factor III: *Problems in case of owner's illness or death: social burden*
            (.91) . . . that a dog would be a problem after my death
            (.84) . . . that a dog would be a problem if I became ill

Factor IV: *Conflicts with partner and risk to children*
            (.79) . . . that a dog would create problems between me and my partner
            (.76) . . . that a dog would put my children at risk

Factor V: *Problems with neighbours and other residents*
            (.74) . . . that a dog would be noisy
            (.68) . . . that a dog would be the cause of trouble between me and my neighbours

Factor VI: *Expenditure of time: dependency, lack of freedom*
            (.84) . . . that I would have to look after the dog in my spare time

Factor VII: *Financial cost*
            (.89) . . . that keeping a dog would be too expensive

Factor VIII: *Accommodation difficulties*
            (.71) . . . that I would have to move if I had a dog

(see note after Table 12)

probability of a dog contributing to the enhancement of quality of life is significantly lower among those who do not own a pet than among dog owners, while the probability that one's quality of life will be seriously impaired by dog ownership is significantly higher.

From the mass of discrete findings we now proceeded to extract the basic general 'cost factors' relating to dog ownership. It emerged that there were hardly any differences between the subject groups in terms of the cost factors as such (see Table 17): the only differences were in perceived probability of incidence.

The perceived disadvantages of dog ownership derive ultimately from restrictions on personal mobility, personal standards of hygiene and cleanliness, the possible acceptance or rejection of a dog by members of one's own family or friends and neighbours, and the problems that can arise with an animal in case of its owner's illness or death. The various subject groups differ somewhat in terms of their precise perceptions of the cost factors: criticism thrives on distinctions, whereas praise is content to generalize.

Table 18 shows what percentage of respondents in the three groups anticipate which particular problems in conjunction with dog ownership. Thus while only 35% of dog owners anticipate a

Table 18   Disadvantages of dog ownership: probability of incidence

	Respondents with dog in household (n = 345)	Respondents with other pets in household (n = 305) (%)	Respondents with no pets in household (n = 280)
Expenditure of time	38	69	75
Restricted freedom of movement	35	79	83
Dirt in the house/flat	23	47	60
Financial cost	19	49	49
Dependency of dog – hence problems in case of owner's illness or death	18	40	48
Problems with the neighbours	18	41	51
Other people put at risk	13	33	44
Transmission of diseases	7	27	34
Difficulties with marital partner	6	25	33

degree of restriction on their personal freedom of movement, the corresponding figure for non pet owners is 83%. Hygiene problems (dirt and the risk of disease transmission) are likewise anticipated by a much higher proportion of subjects in the latter group.

However, in order to explain human behaviour it is not enough simply to look at the so-called cost factors in isolation. What matters is the relationship between 'costs' on the one hand and 'benefits' on the other – or in other words, the overall psychology evaluation.

9 Overall psychological evaluation of dog ownership

Having examined the meaning and relative significance of the personal advantages and disadvantages of dog ownership, we may now proceed to calculate an overall value reflecting the balance of these factors (for details of calculation see Appendix).

This value is an index of the extent to which dog ownership is perceived as a positive or negative experience. In other words, it is possible to express a person's overall perception and evaluation of a dog in terms of a single index value. This value reflects the probability of incidence of all the possible benefit and cost factors of dog ownership. A positive value expresses the extent of the contribution that a dog makes to a person's well-being – and hence quality of life. At the same time the index value must be seen as a crucial motivating factor in dog ownership. A person with a high positive score is either a dog owner already or must be viewed as a potential future owner. Self-evidently, anyone who believes that a dog can contribute positively to his life will give thought to the possibility of acquiring a dog. By the same token, of course, a dog owner with a negative score, i.e. one who sees more disadvantages than advantages in dog ownership, must be regarded as someone who is potentially likely to get rid of his dog.

Table 19 shows the mean scores for the three subject groups,

Table 19 Overall psychological evaluation of dog ownership

	Respondents with dog in household (n = 345)	Respondents with other pets in household (n = 305) (%)	Respondents with no pets in household (n = 280)
Positive score (0 to +48)	89	54	32
Mean score	+15	+11	+9
Negative score (0 to −48)	11	46	68
Mean score	−3	−8	−10
Mean overall group score	12.7	0.8	−3.7

together with the distribution of positive and negative scores within each group.

As one would expect, the highest overall mean group score is achieved by dog owners (+12.7), while the lowest overall score (−3.7) is returned by non pet owners. However, the findings show that persons with positive scores are to be found in all three groups. It is also apparent that the mean scores for 'positive' and 'negative' subjects differ quite significantly from group to group, indicating that the probability of dog ownership increases with the rise in positive index values.

Positive attitudes to dogs are not therefore confined to those persons who currently own a dog. While positive scores were recorded for 89% of dog owners, the corresponding figures for the other two groups – owners of other pets and non pet owners – were 54% and 32% respectively.

The fact that a not insignificant proportion of non-owners arrive at an overall positive verdict calls for a word of explanation. A comparison with non-smokers, for example, shows that more than 90% of this group evaluate smoking negatively. At the same time non-smokers are far more critical in their evaluation of smoking, recording significantly higher negative scores. In other words, a dog is perceived as being a more beneficial and salutory source of pleasure than tobacco, which is frequently a target for public disapproval. Smokers are seen to be flouting the health norms of their society.

It should also be pointed out that not all dog owners recorded a positive score. While 89% were positive, the remaining 11% came out marginally on the negative side. This means that there exists a special category of 'undecided' or 'unstable' dog owners, who experience some impairment of their quality of life through dog ownership. They feel restricted in their personal freedom of movement and hence dependent. However, negative scores in such cases are also related to the fact that the anticipated benefits of dog ownership are considered less likely of attainment by these respondents than they are among those who score positively.

From this it may be generally concluded that despite a positive basic attitude, and despite clear evidence that a dog can contribute significantly to the enhancement of personal quality of life, the *extent* of that contribution is not sufficient to ensure the continuing stabilization of the relationship between man and dog.

'Unstable' dog owners and non dog owners share the same difficulties with regard to the perceived restrictions on individual freedom and mobility.

In the case of dog owners with negative scores it should also be pointed out that, whereas their expectations of a dog's contribution to their own well-being are relatively slight, they are particularly sensitive to the cost factors of dog ownership.

Table 20 places the distribution of positive and negative scores in an overall demographic context. The first point of interest to note is that one or more dogs are kept by 3.2 million households in West Germany (out of a total of 25.3 million households), creating a total dog population of 3.3 million. This means that a total of 7.5 million West Germans live in households where there is also a dog. If we then take *all* the persons whose overall evaluation of dogs is positive, we arrive at a combined total figure of 22.3 million – or very nearly half the West German population. These are all persons who associate a personal 'reward value' with dogs and feel a certain affection for them.

Table 20   Distribution of dog ownership in the West German population

	Respondents with dog in household	Respondents with other pets in household	Respondents with no pets in household
	7.5	11.4	29.3
	No. of persons and households (in millions)		
Positive overall score:			
Households	2.9	3.0	5.3
Persons	6.7	6.2	9.4
Negative overall score:			
Households	0.3	2.6	11.2
Persons	0.8	5.2	19.9

The significance of a dog for personal well-being and quality of life has hitherto been inferred from the perceived likely contribution of a dog to the satisfaction of human needs and aspirations. If the question is put to people directly, however – leaving aside for the moment any methodological objections that one might have – we find that a remarkable 48% of dog owners, and 16% of non pet owners, are prepared to claim that a dog has a significant contribution to make to the enhancement of individual quality of life. This is supported by a series of further findings reflecting a positive overall evaluation of the man–dog relationship. Any questions relating to general or specific satisfaction with life, well-being or personal self-assessment elicited positive responses from these subjects in all the following areas:

- General satisfaction with life.
- Cheerful attitude to life.
- Good relations with colleagues and neighbours.
- Fun and enjoyment in life.
- Satisfaction with one's job, family and leisure activities.
- Inner mental harmony.
- Openness to others, no problems about starting up a conversation with others, expressing one's own point of view and taking the initiative to act.
- Self-acceptance, self-assurance.
- Socially desirable characteristics, e.g. gregarious, affable, cheerful, responsible, contented, sociable, generous.

There is no doubt, therefore, that a dog has a very useful contribution to make in terms of encouraging the development of personal contentment and well-being, based on positive self-appraisal and self-assurance. If pets were *not* capable of exercising this kind of psychological influence on human personality, there would be no basis whatsoever for their various pedagogic or therapeutic applications. But the relationship between man and dog is one of mutual dependency *and* mutual influence. Dogs are one contributory factor in human personality development.

Other psychological factors affecting dog ownership

Experiences with animals

Animals as such are a topic of interest to many people, regardless of whether they own one themselves. Nearly all of us have had some kind of personal experience with animals. What is more, we seem able to recall these experiences in great detail many years after the event – proof enough of the intrinsic significance of such incidents in our lives. Positive recollections of such experiences are by no means confined to those of us who own a dog or other animal. Indeed, it would appear that positive encounters with animals – particularly pets – are an essential part of normal human development.

We begin by looking at past experiences with dogs, then move on to consider experiences with other kinds of animals.

Experiences with dogs

Table 21 shows that 47% of persons with other pets in the household and 36% of those with no pets are able to report some kind of past experience with dogs. Certain differences emerge, however, in terms of the way the various subject groups evaluate these experiences.

Table 21   Quality of past experiences with dogs

	Recollections of experiences with dogs		
	Respondents with dog in household (n = 345)	Respondents with other pets in household (n = 143) (%)	Respondents with no pets in household (n = 92)
Positive experiences	73	47	36
Positive and negative experiences in approx. equal proportions	26	34	49
Primarily negative experiences	1	19	15

Not surprisingly, the proportion of subjects with nothing but positive experiences of dogs to report is significantly higher among dog owners than in the other two groups. But this is not to say that such persons are not represented in these groups, where they account for 47% and 36% of respondents respectively. Those with no pets differ from those with dogs or other pets primarily in terms of the frequency with which they report a combination of positive and negative experiences. This 'both/and' response reflects a measure of uncertainty, which in turn furnishes a poor psychological basis for reinforcing the subject's limited desire to acquire a dog. This could only occur if the 'input' of positive information, experiences and expectations were to be significantly increased. Primarily negative experiences with dogs are reported by 19% of those with other pets, and by 15% of those with no pets at all.

To illustrate the kind of positive experiences identified by subjects, we have included a representative selection of verbatim
reports:

- Childhood experiences

  ' . . . when the dog had puppies I always played with them; we
  had a special litter box for the dog, and I always used to rush
  over and see if they'd been born yet. I was always so thrilled
  when she had her puppies . . . '

  ' . . . there was an Alsatian in the farmyard, and I used to spend
  a lot of time with him; my best friend had a dog, and I played
  with him a lot too; we often used to play with the dog, get him
  to jump in the water, and all that; we used to organize special
  dog races; we used to tease the neighbours' little dachshund,
  and he would chase after us; the dog was 'one of the gang' when
  we went off on some adventure, and we thought we were great
  trappers or pioneers; my grandfather often let me take his dog
  for a walk; I often went walking with the dogs from the
  neighbourhood; we used to dress up the dog in my grandma's
  skirts and blouses; we used to put a hat on the dog; he was good
  to play with, he didn't mind what you did; he was wonderful to
  cuddle and stroke; there was always something to do with him;
  I liked playing with him and stroking him . . . '

- Going for walks together (dog owners only)

  ' . . . when we go for a walk together; "walkies" is always such
  fun, when the dog meets his friends; he really loves to go
  "walkies"; long walks; going out for walks every day; he looks
  good when he's out walking; I like the way he moves; he's a real
  companion for me . . . '

- Homecoming from work (dog owners only)

  ' . . . every day when I get home from the office the dog is so
  pleased to see me; when I get home in the evening and the dog
  is pleased to see me . . . '

  ' . . . he barks when he hears me coming, I've hardly turned the
  key in the door before he's jumping up, so pleased to see me. It's
  nice for him to have me home – and nice for me to have such a
  warm welcome . . . '

● Holiday memories (dog owners only)

' . . . on holiday together, when I had plenty of time for my "baby"; when I went on holiday to Vienna, where dogs have to wear a muzzle by law, my dachshund had to wear a muzzle – he looked so funny; the best times were in the vacations, when we went swimming with him; we went for lovely walks together on holiday, and slept in the same tent together . . . '

' . . . on holiday I can devote lots of time to him, we do lots of nice things together; on holiday is when I most appreciate having such a faithful friend . . . '

● Behaviour of dog (dog owners only)

' . . . when he clowns around; at Christmas he sniffed out his sausage in no time; the first time he saw a Christmas tree with lights on he ran out of the room and peeped round the door; in a hotel once he collected up all the shoes in the corridor and put them outside our door; whenever there was a vocalist on TV he used to sing along with her; after his ear infection he always flattened his ears whenever he saw me with a cotton bud . . . '

' . . . we laugh ourselves silly when he sits in the window and stares at the neighbour's cat; as soon as he sees his ball he runs off to fetch it, even though I haven't thrown it yet. It's so funny . . . '

● Looking after a dog (dog owners only)

' . . . we once had a dog to look after for two weeks, that was good fun; I always used to take a big bone for the neighbours' dog; a friend once left his dog with us while he was away, and we had some good times with it . . .'

Those were some of the positive recollections. An insight into the negative experiences with dogs recalled by other subjects is furnished by the selection of typical replies reprinted below:

● Vicious, aggressive behaviour by dogs (non dog owners only)

' . . . I was once attacked by a dog when I was out walking, suddenly he came out of the bushes, jumped up at me and bit me in the arm; I was playing with a dog in the street, and all at once he bit me . . . '

- Death or illness of dog (current and former dog owners)

' . . . I remember the time when the dog died, towards the end he just kind of vegetated; the death of my dog was a severe shock to me, I can still remember how I cried all night; I was really sad when he died, I cried my eyes out; the dog was very ill at the end, they had to put him to sleep; the dog once ate something poisonous and became very ill . . . '

  - Regular reponsibilities (current and former dog owners)

' . . . I have to take him out even when the weather's bad; in winter it's really too cold to go outside, but you have no choice; always having to take him out walking in the cold; in the evenings he's constantly in and out of the house, and you have to go with him, of course . . . '

- Excessive noise (current and former dog owners)

' . . . he barked and howled a lot; when the dog barks in the night and disturbs the other tenants; the dog always howled a lot at night; if you went out in the evening he always started to howl . . . '

- Expenditure of time (current and former dog owners)

' . . . the dog gets on my nerves when he wants to play and I don't have the time; we all need a bit of peace and quiet, but the dog never leaves you alone . . . '

- Problems in case of own illness (current and former dog owners)

' . . . when I was ill I had lots of problems with the dog; when I broke my leg I found it hard to take him out for walks – there were times I would rather have been without a dog . . . '

Negative experiences with dogs tend to focus around bites in the case of non dog owners, whereas dog owners, current as well as former, mention such things as having to be there all the time for a dog, i.e. the need to accept constraints on their own behaviour, as well as the need to risk a certain amount of conflict with other people.

Experiences with other animals

Since human encounters with animals are by no means confined to dogs, we were also concerned to analyse subjects' experiences with other animals. Here again considerable differences emerged between the three subject groups. Fifty-nine per cent of dog owners, 66% of respondents with other pets and 29% of respondents with no pets are able to recall experiences with other animals. As Table 22 shows, experiences of a predominantly negative kind are scarcely mentioned at all – although it is also clear that a significantly greater proportion of persons who currently own a pet of some kind, including dogs, are able to recall pleasant experiences and encounters with animals from their past lives than respondents who do not keep pets. In fact only 59% of the latter group associate exclusively positive memories with animals, whereas 41% recall a roughly equal number of positive and negative experiences.

Table 22   Quality of past experiences with animals

	Recollections of experiences with other animals (excluding dogs)		
	Respondents with dog in household (n = 204)	Respondents with other pets in household (n = 201)	Respondents with no pets in household (n = 81)
		(%)	
Positive experiences	73	71	59
Positive and negative experiences in approx. equal proportions	24	27	41
Primarily negative experiences	3	2	–

In interpreting these findings, we need to take account of the problems of subjective evaluation – i.e. the way in which different people respond differently to the same events and incidents – particularly when we come to analyse cause and effect. It has already been established that dog ownership – and hence non-ownership – do not lend themselves to a simple cause-and-effect explanation. Given that experiences with animals in the course of one's development are seen as factors that help to co-determine one's attitudes and behaviour towards pets, the data revealed by this survey merely confirm the existence of a positive correlation between experiences with animals, a love of animals and pet ownership, but to infer a direct causal connection between these three things would not be justified.

However, it *is* possible to draw certain conclusions of a psychological/pedagogical nature, for it is undoubtedly correct to say that the mediation of positive experiences with the natural world and animal kingdom is a vital prerequisite for the development of a love of nature and animals. Children and adults who do not learn to study and experience nature and animals at first hand will hardly learn to love them – which is essential if they are to develop a sense of personal responsibility for the environment. Once again, the best way to characterize these positive experiences with animals is to quote some of the actual statements made by respondents.

• Feeding animals

' . . . in the winter we always put food out for the birds; as a child I was allowed to help on the farm in the holidays, feeding the animals and mucking out; my grandparents lived on the outskirts of town and kept rabbits, we loved to feed them when we were visiting as children, we thought the bunnies were great; I nearly always had a lump of sugar for the horses in my pockets . . . '

• Playing with animals

' . . . loved playing with the animal; when I was little we spent our holidays on a farm, and there was a cockerel there called Joseph. I used to carry him around and give him rides in the pram; the cat was great to play with; we used to organize circus shows with cats, rabbits and dogs . . . '

• Observing animals

' . . . watching animals; I like watching animals, horses and cats when they are moving; the cats were the nicest ones to look at, they were so elegant; I have happy memories of bird-watching at the bird sanctuary on Sylt; in Ceylon I watched pairs of elephants bathing in the river at dawn . . . '

- At the circus or zoo

  ' . . . we often went to the zoo; I liked the big animals especially, I knew all the animals by name; I went to the zoo as often as I could; I've always loved animals; so I often went to the zoo as a child; for a while back then I even wanted to work with horses as a groom; once when we went to the zoo we took a lipstick with us and gave it to the monkeys – they painted themselves with it, and the next day the keeper told us off; when the polar bears in the zoo had cubs my sister and I were allowed to help rear them . . . '

- Fun and games with animals

  ' . . . my cat was always larking about; the bird used to dive-bomb my train set; the bird sometimes landed on your plate when you were eating; it was so funny when the bird flew straight into the washing-up water; the bird sometimes stole things off the table; the hamster was funny, he used to race around the top of the table at high speed; one Christmas the cat carefully removed all the decorations from the tree . . . '

- Birth and development of young

  ' . . . when she had puppies; I always enjoyed helping out at the birth; I loved to see the babies; whenever the cat had kittens; the little kittens were a lovely sight; once the cat had her kittens in my bed . . . '

This catalogue of positive experiences and memories needs to be balanced by some reference to the negative experiences recalled by subjects. The latter fall broadly into two categories: injuries inflicted on humans by animals, and the natural death or slaughter of an animal or pet.

- Injuries inflicted by an animal

  '. . . I was scratched by a cat; I once milked a goat that was tied to a fence. All of a sudden it kicked out and broke my leg; I was injured once when the horse reared up and threw me; the neighbouring farmer once got kicked in the head by his work-horse, and died of his injuries . . .'

- Slaughter of animals

'. . . I remember animals being slaughtered at home, I was always so sorry for them, it was often a real bloodbath; we once had a pig, and when it was fully-grown we gave it to a neighbour to slaughter, and they persuaded me to stir the blood, and as I stirred I couldn't stop crying; the horrible squealing when they slaughtered the pig; the slaughter of hares, to this day I can't bear to eat roast hare . . .'

- Death of a pet

'. . . I remember when the poor thing died; I felt dreadful whenever one of my pets died; the death of an animal saddens me greatly; I was very sad when he got run over . . .'

Positive and negative memories alike both show how emotionally charged such experiences are, and how deeply a person who has had such experiences is affected and moved by them. And it is precisely because of their profound emotional impact that these incidents have such a lasting influence on a person's subsequent behaviour and life-style.

Influence of the parental home on dog ownership

The effect of experiences with animals on the development of one's attitudes and behaviour towards animals – irrespective of whether one has grown up with a pet in the parental home – has already been established. The time has now come to ask to what extent this natural, unquestioning association with animals in the parental home has any explanation value for one's own subsequent behaviour.

Both the qualitative pilot study and the representative study show that a child's early exposure to pets by his parents has a definite influence on pet ownership in adult life. As can be seen from Table 23, 65% of current non pet owners come from homes where there were no pets. The corresponding ratios for the other two subject groups are significantly lower. The influence of the parental home is seen not only in the fact that one does or does not keep a pet: it also affects the *kind* of pet one chooses to keep.

Nearly half the dog owners who no longer live in the parental home report that their parents kept a dog; in the case of those correspondents who now own pets other than a dog, the figure is only 26%.

Table 23   Pets in the parental home

	(No longer resident in parental home)		
	Respondents with dog in household (n = 272)	Respondents with other pets in household (n = 229)	Respondents with no pets in household (n = 255)
	(%)		
	(multiple replies possible)		
Dog	47	26	16
Cat	31	31	18
Budgerigar	13	18	6
Canary	6	7	5
Other cage birds (excl. pigeons)	3	2	3
Other pets, e.g. hamster, guinea pig, tropical fish, etc.	7	9	4
None	40	45	65

The degree of importance attached to a dog in later life is undoubtedly determined in part by the experience of the parental home. A person who has discovered the joys of dog ownership as a child is obviously more likely to acquire a dog in adult life. In this connection it is also useful to see what the respondents' replies tell us about the *quality* of the relationship between humans and dogs in the parental home. We need to know, for example, whether the respondent was directly involved in looking after the pet as a child. And we need to know what dogs and other pets actually *meant* to the respondent at a very personal level – how 'important' they were, in other words.

If we look now at subjects in terms not of whether they currently own a pet, but of whether they evaluate dog ownership positively or negatively, a correlation with their childhood experiences does emerge. Specifically, persons who no longer live with their parents, but who state that they were actively involved in looking after a dog or cat in the parental home (this does not apply to pets other than dogs or cats), *and* that the pet was especially important to them as a child, are now among those who, after weighing up all the pros and cons of dog ownership, evaluate possible ownership positively. Conversely, those without such a history of personal involvement are numbered among those who evaluate possible ownership negatively. Here again, the differences between the two groups are readily apparent.

So as far as later attitudes to pets are concerned, what matters is not only that one grew up with a pet as a child, but also – and more crucially – that one assumed a degree of responsibility for the animal, helping to feed and care for it and actively interrelating with it. Having experience *of* animals is one thing: sharing experience *with* animals is something else again. Before animals can have a lastingly beneficial influence on our well-being, we must learn to take them seriously – and value our relationships with them.

Relative importance of dogs compared with alternative aspirations and behavioural options

The individual's psychological evaluation of dog ownership is always influenced in part by the relative importance attached to other desirable behavioural alternatives, i.e. the so-called comparison level of alternatives. Unfortunately it was not possible, within the framework of the present study, to carry out a detailed psychological evaluation of those alternatives. Instead we established a provisional ranking order, ranging from 'least important' to 'most important', for a set of possible aspirations. Our purpose was to ascertain the importance that different persons attach to a dog relative to other objects of gratification. The resulting pattern of preferences is charted in Fig. 24.

It is hardly surprising that the desire for interpersonal intimacy, i.e. for relationships with persons who are totally reliable, sympathetic, understanding and trusting, should come top of the list for all three subject groups. Dogs are then ranked second by dog owners, while the other two subject groups put them last, i.e. dogs are considered least important in comparison with other desirable objects. But this does not mean – as we saw from an overall psychological evaluation of dog ownership – that dogs have *no* positive associations for these persons. It simply means that these persons regard the potential contribution of a dog to their own quality of life as relatively insignificant at this point in time, i.e. they attach more importance to the available alternatives.

As already stated, the body of data was analysed not just in terms of the three subject groups (dog owners, owners of other

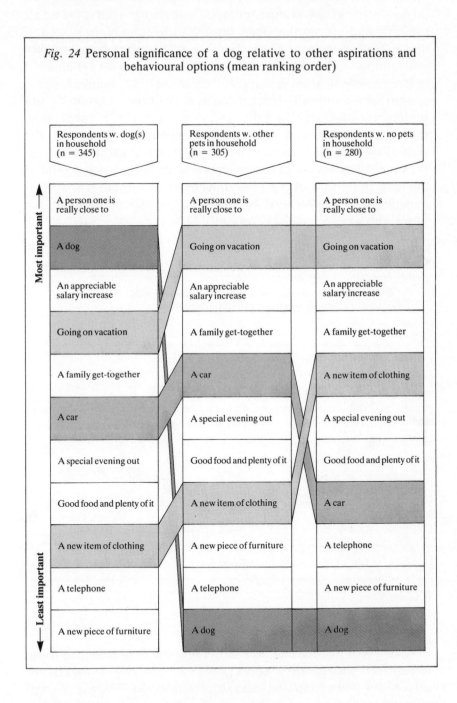

Fig. 24 Personal significance of a dog relative to other aspirations and behavioural options (mean ranking order)

pets, non pet owners), but also in terms of psychological type based on positive/negative evaluation of dog ownership. That is to say, all subjects who scored positively on dog ownership were placed in one group, while those who scored negatively were placed in a second group – regardless of whether they currently own a pet or not.

If we now look at these two groups in terms of the number of persons in each group who place a dog at each of the 11 points on the preference rating scale (see Fig. 25), we get a clearer picture of how the groups differ with regard to the personal significance (or centrality) of a dog. The results are statistically attested. Among the range of behavioural alternatives offered here, a dog was rated the least important of the 11 options by 45% of those who scored negatively on dog ownership, while the corresponding figure for those who scored positively was only 12%.

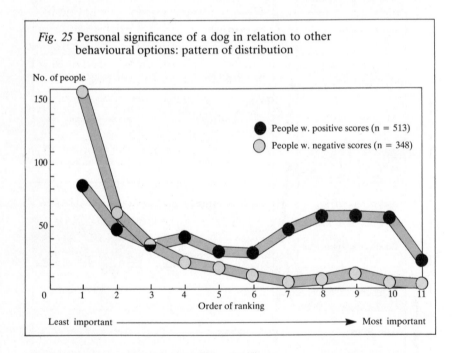

Fig. 25 Personal significance of a dog in relation to other behavioural options: pattern of distribution

Analysis of the findings also shows that the significance of a dog for subjects with positive scores (and indeed for dog owners themselves) may vary from one individual to the next. The psychological pilot study helps us to define these differences by highlighting the specific views of dog owners on the significance of dogs in their daily routine, at weekends and on vacation. First, some quotations that indicate a high degree of centrality:

● The dog as the focal point of daily routine:

'. . . when I get up in the mornings the first thing I do is say hello to my dog, and we spend half an hour playing; in the mornings he has his breakfast, then goes out in the garden, or else we go for a walk together; as soon as I get up in the morning I let him out into the garden, where he does his business, then he trots around after me, in the bathroom he lies on the floor and sleeps, when I'm preparing breakfast he lies in his basket, when all the family has got up he sits next to the breakfast table and waits for titbits, then we go shopping together and I give him something to eat just before ten, then he goes out in the garden, plays around and barks, at lunch he sits or lies next to the table, after lunch we go for a walk together, then he can do what he likes, rush around to his heart's content, after his walk he has a sleep, in the evening I give him a big meal, quite often I play with him, sometimes we go for another walk, in the dark he becomes very alert and keeps watch, he sleeps at the foot of my bed . . .'

● The dog as the focal point of the weekend:

'. . . when the weather's nice we drive out into the country, to get some good clean air in our lungs; we go walking a lot at the weekends; if we go out anywhere at the weekend we always make sure it's somewhere we can take the dog, we even take him along to the restaurant; when he's with me I only ever go to bars and restaurants where dogs are also allowed in; on Saturdays and Sundays I take him along to the dog club at eight in the morning, at the club the dogs are properly trained . . .'

● The dog as the focal point of the vacation trip:

'. . . we always take the dog with us, in fact we always make sure, when choosing our holiday destination, that it's somewhere where dogs are allowed; the dog usually comes with us; I take my dog with me on holidays, usually up to the mountains, there's a guest house where I normally stay every year, he always stays there with me, he really feels at home there; we like to take the dog with us on holiday, people come up and speak to you, you quickly make friends, it's good fun . . .'

These remarks confirm once again that persons who accord a dog a central place in their life do so because they believe, as dog owners, that a dog contributes positively to their quality of life. At the same time there are other dog owners for whom a dog is not automatically the most important among the available alternatives. To illustrate the point, here are a few further verbatim comments:

- Limited importance of the dog in daily routine

'. . . I take him walking for half an hour in the morning, the rest of the day the dog is alone in the apartment, it works very well, he's been used to that ever since he was a puppy, in the evening I take the dog out for a walk again, if I don't have anything else to do; there are some days when he has to be content with an hour's walk; I keep my dogs in a kennel in the garden, in the evening I clean out the kennel, then take the dogs walking for an hour. Then I feed them – and that's it for the day; I take the dog out in the evening, though my husband could do it just as easily – in fact it's rather a sore point between us; after breakfast I take the dog out for a walk, then drop him off at my mother's while I go to work. I pick him up in the afternoon and we go for a walk, then I give him something to eat a little later on, when I'm doing the housework I sometimes play with the dog a bit . . .'

- Limited importance of the dog at weekends

'. . . the dog can be a bit of a nuisance at the weekends; luckily we have nice neighbours who don't mind looking after the dog if we want to go and visit friends; he sometimes gets in the way a bit and makes us late when we want to go out . . .'

- Limited importance of the dog on vacations

'. . . we leave him with my parents; I leave him with my son and grandchildren; my mother looks after the dog; we usually leave him with his previous owner, we know he's in good hands there; we put him in the boarding kennels . . .'

The evidence indicates that the personal significance of a dog may vary from one dog owner to another. What is more, even for one and the same dog owner a dog may have a different importance at the weekend than he does in the normal daily routine. The same ambivalence does not appear to apply to vacations, where dog owners either plan their holiday entirely around the dog or else make clear alternative arrangements, leaving the dog with friends, neighbours, or a boarding kennel.

Our findings on the centrality of a dog in relation to other aspirations and behavioural options have shown that this is undoubtedly a further determining factor in the decision-making process that can lead either to the acquisition or to the rejection of a dog. Here it is important to point out once again that rejection is a real possibility even in cases where the overall psychological evaluation of dog ownership is positive. In order to maximize the explanation and prediction value of our model, we need to ask what ancillary factors have to obtain – and what relative importance has to be attached to those factors – before a person decides to acquire or not acquire a dog, regardless of whether they score positively or negatively on the prospect of dog ownership? Although these scores have a considerable explanation and prediction value for actual behaviour – acquisition or non-acquisition of a dog – this does not apply to the whole of the sample interviewed here. Those so-called ancillary factors and their diagnosis provide us with the means to improve the explanation and prediction value still further, thanks in no small part to the comparison level of alternatives.

To summarize, we can say that a person who scores positively overall on the prospect of dog ownership, and who rates a dog highly in terms of personal significance and desirability for his own life-style, can be expected to acquire a dog *if*:

1. he grew up with a dog;
2. the experiences and memories he associates with animals in general and dogs in particular are predominantly positive;
3. as a child he had a close personal relationship with dogs or cats; and
4. he assumed some measure of personal responsibility for the dog during childhood.

10 Preconceptions and prejudices: dogs and society

Dogs are a recognized topic of private and public debate. They can be the subject of much controversy, the ostensible cause of inter-personal conflict and hostility: equally, they may be a source of new friendships. People are categorized and judged according to whether they are dog owners or not. The relationship between dogs and society is essentially reflected in the self-appraisal and appraisal by others of dog owners and non dog owners, i.e. in social prejudices (Bergler, 1966).

In our earlier discussion of the psychological cost factors and the possible obstacles to dog ownership, reference was made to the possibility of conflict between dog owners and non dog owners. We shall now proceed to a closer examination of that relationship, as reflected in the reciprocal assessments of the various groups involved, their self-appraisal and the supposed opinions of others. Each subject interviewed was asked to state his attitude to dog owners as a group and non dog owners as a group (i.e. self-image and other image), and also to say how he thought his own particular group – dog owners or non dog owners – was seen and evaluated by the other group (supposed other image). These patterns of assessment are important for what they tell us about the social distance between the various groups, i.e. the extent to which dog owners believe they are understood and accepted – or indeed rejected and disliked – by non-owners. If a person is convinced that others see him exactly as he sees himself – i.e. if self-image and supposed other image correspond, or at least resemble each other closely – then relationships are likely to be amicable. People believe they understand each other, they are approachable, and conflict is unlikely. But it is a very different story if a person supposes that others view him in a negative light, i.e. if his own self-image is more positive than the supposed other image. Regardless of the actual truth contained in such suppositions (and this point was verified in the course of the present study), apparent discrepancies of this kind between self-image and supposed other image are more than enough to distance one from the other person, to view him with suspicion – and hence to be somewhat unfriendly and reserved in one's own behaviour.

In many ways our perception of reality is governed by prejudices of this kind. Not that we care to look too closely at our own prejudices: they are far too convenient, far too useful for that, helping us as they do to make the world a less complicated place by simplified characterization and typology. And if these prejudices result in hostility and conflict, we automatically blame the prejudices of others – which we take to be misguided – rather than our own, which we regard as entirely wholesome and justified.

It was already apparent in our psychological pilot study that dog owners view their own group (and hence of course themselves) in a very positive light. Their image of the typical dog owner is marked by a number of very pronounced positive characteristics such as sociability, tolerance, responsibility, gregariousness and personal contentment.

The typical non dog owner, on the other hand, is viewed by dog owners as a rather unlikeable person, self-centred, emotionally distant and intent on self-gratification at any price. Needless to say, the typical non dog owner is also thought to have no love for animals – a characteristic which serves to make him even less lovable.

The mechanisms at work behind these prejudices are best studied through the words of the respondents themselves. We begin with some statements on self-image, i.e. the way dog owners themselves see the 'typical' dog owner:

- Animal-loving

  '. . . there are only certain people who can keep a dog, but it has nothing to do with their age or the type of work they do. The one thing they must have is a love of animals; he must be an animal lover; an animal-loving person; he loves animals; likes animals; has a soft spot for animals . . .'

- Nature-loving

  '. . . loves nature; is interested in nature; people who like dogs are more interested in nature, they live outside the city and have a garden; nature is something very important to him; he likes living close to nature; somebody who enjoys being out in the fresh air; a nature-loving person who likes to be outside . . .'

- Likes going for walks

  '. . . he likes being outside, going for walks; he likes walking . . .'

- Emotional, sensitive

  '. . . always sympathizes with other people; is emotional; sensitive; they are very lovable people; they have a kind heart; can empathize well with other people; has compassion; is not cold and unemotional like so many people . . .'

- Sociable, gregarious

  '. . . I know lots of dog owners, they are all very sociable; dog owners are gregarious by nature; dog owners are a really sociable crowd . . .'

It is quite clear from this that dog owners see themselves in the socially desirable role of friendly, affable people, whom others cannot fail to like.

By contrast, the 'typical' non dog owner tends to be viewed in a rather negative light by dog owners, as the following comments show:

- Egoistic

  '. . . they're egoists with a desire for freedom, or rather they're egocentric; they're egoistic; they're more egoistic than other people; they are not very interested in the needs of others; they don't care about anybody or anything; they only think about their own interests . . .'

- Not animal-loving

  '. . . they can't relate to animals; they're not animal-loving; don't like animals; don't really understand animals; they're only friendly with people who don't own animals; have no feelings for animals; animals don't mean anything to them, they can't relate to them; they don't have any love for animals . . .'

- No rapport with nature

  '. . . is much more interested in technical things than nature; not much feeling for nature, more practically-minded; they don't much like going for walks; they have no rapport with nature; nature doesn't mean much to them; they couldn't care less about nature . . .'

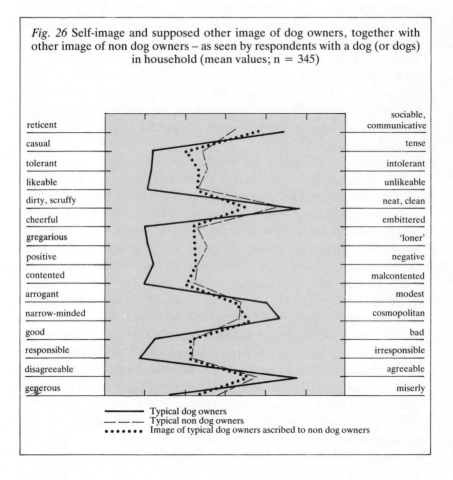

Fig. 26 Self-image and supposed other image of dog owners, together with other image of non dog owners – as seen by respondents with a dog (or dogs) in household (mean values; n = 345)

reticent	sociable, communicative
casual	tense
tolerant	intolerant
likeable	unlikeable
dirty, scruffy	neat, clean
cheerful	embittered
gregarious	'loner'
positive	negative
contented	malcontented
arrogant	modest
narrow-minded	cosmopolitan
good	bad
responsible	irresponsible
disagreeable	agreeable
generous	miserly

Typical dog owners
Typical non dog owners
Image of typical dog owners ascribed to non dog owners

All the characteristics that make a person appear friendly and likeable in the eyes of dog owners are lacking in those persons who do not own a dog. In fact, the person who emerges from these descriptions is somebody for whom it would be very difficult to feel sympathy and affection.

The picture that began to emerge in our qualitative findings is confirmed by the results of the representative study. Figure 26 (in which all the results are statistically highly significant) shows that dog owners see themselves as members of a minority group, who live in a certain state of conflict with the majority – and hence with society as a whole. Compared with themselves, they see the typical non dog owner as less likeable, more sober and matter-of-fact, more cautious, and something of an egoist in his behaviour. Socially desirable characteristics such as sociability, tolerance, responsibility, gregariousness and personal contentment are essential components of their own self-image. The typical dog owner sees himself as contented, cheerful, responsible, likeable and tolerant, someone who is casual and affable in his manner, neat and agreeable in his habits. In short, the self-image of the dog owner differs in a very positive way from the image he has of the typical non dog owner.

Equally revealing are the replies given by dog owners when asked to speculate on the image that non dog owners had of dog owners as a group. Dog owners clearly believe that non dog owners view the typical dog owner in very much the same way that they – dog owners – view non-owners. Or, to put it another way, dog owners believe that each group has a similarly hostile image of the other, that there are clear differences of 'character' between the two groups, and that there is little love lost between them. Whether this assumption is correct is something we shall consider in due course below. For the present, however, we shall proceed on the basis of the dog owner's belief that society is negatively prejudiced against him, that despite payment of the dog licence fee he is not automatically accepted by his fellows and is thus forced into the position of a social minority group. Since his behaviour is partly determined by these expectations, social conflict is likely. At the very least he will approach his non dog owning fellows with feelings of caution, scepticism and even a degree of uncertainty. It is entirely possible that such attitudes and feelings will give rise to a rejection and condemnation of other people, and even, in extreme cases, to overtly hostile behaviour in the form of verbal aggression. However, non dog owners are by no means as hostile to dog owners as dog owners themselves are inclined to believe (largely, no doubt, because they tend to generalize on the basis of isolated incidents). The negative prejudices which they believe to be so widespread are encountered only rarely in real life.

This fact is borne out by the findings charted in Fig. 27. The data here are based on a further stage of analysis, whereby all persons

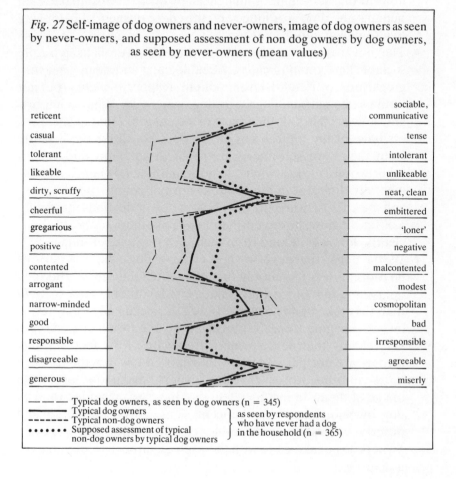

Fig. 27 Self-image of dog owners and never-owners, image of dog owners as seen by never-owners, and supposed assessment of non dog owners by dog owners, as seen by never-owners (mean values)

in the 'other pets' and 'no pets' groups who had at some stage in the past owned a dog were excluded from the reckoning to form a new group of 'never-owners'. In this way we were able to rule out any distortion of the results arising from the fact that current non-owners might have owned a dog themselves at some stage. Plotting the results in the form of a graph makes a number of points immediately apparent:

● The typological self-assessments of dog owners and of persons who have never owned a dog are significantly different in so far as the first group describes and evaluates itself more positively overall. The group's self-image, in other words, is an unequivocally positive one. However, the findings do not permit us to say how far that self-image is influenced by the relationship between humans and dogs – or indeed by the consciousness of belonging to a so-called minority group.

- The never-owner also describes himself overall as typically sociable and communicative, likeable, neat and clean, cheerful, gregarious, contented, cosmopolitan, responsible, etc. – but not to the same marked degree as dog owners do. What is important, however, is that the image or psychogram that never-owners have of the typical dog owner does not differ significantly from their own self-image in any of these characteristics. In other words, never-owners do not regard dog owners as fundamentally different in kind, but as normal people 'just like you and me'. Those who currently have a dog in the household take a different view, however: their image of others is a hostile one, clearly different in kind from their own positive self-image.

- We have seen that never-owners evaluate dog owners as persons no more or less favourably than they rate themselves. But they do assume that dog owners take a less favourable view of *them* than they take of dog owners. If we ask, specifically, how never-owners imagine they are perceived by dog owners, it emerges very clearly that never-owners are aware of the fact that dog owners are not particularly well-disposed towards them. They know, in other words, that dog owners have a kind of hostile image of them. In fact they feel that they are misunderstood by dog owners, labelled as reticent, tense, even intolerant and miserly – socially undesirable characteristics which never-owners do *not* associate with themselves, either as individuals or as a group.

It certainly seems, therefore, that relationships between persons who own a dog and those who do not are somewhat problematic. On the one hand we have dog owners, who find non-owners rather disagreeable and see no good reason why they should have anything to do with such people. On the other hand we have non-owners, who for their part do not harbour any negative prejudices about dog owners, but who know very well that dog owners are negatively disposed towards *them*. Consequently there is no compelling psychological reason for either party to take the initiative and attempt a *rapprochement*, perhaps even sharing positive experiences with an animal. But whereas dog owners view non-owners with feelings of uncertainty *and* a certain degree of antipathy, non-owners tend to be more neutrally distanced in their attitude to dog owners, based on the assumption that the latter want nothing to do with them. So a certain amount of groundwork is necessary before both sides can enter into a dialogue. And in particular, dog owners must realize that non-owners are generally more tolerant, friendly and open in their attitude towards dog owners than dog owners themselves suppose.

Since dog owners expect to be perceived negatively by others, so that a process of social distancing occurs, the problem arises of inappropriate social behaviour vis-à-vis non dog owners. Non dog owners view dog owners in a more friendly light than the latter suppose. Put very simply, dog owners have more friends than they imagine. Here again, therefore, natural and uncomplicated human relations are thwarted by the presence of negative prejudices. Indirectly this creates problems for dog owners with other residents and tenants, neighbours, friends and acquaintances – problems that are entirely avoidable. We sometimes say that a person 'is his own worst enemy': and indeed, our own prejudices – and the resulting breakdown in communication – are often the biggest obstacle to our own well-being.

11   Psychological groups and types of dog owner

The large amount of data at our disposal enabled us to carry out a series of further analytical procedures. In particular we drew on another representative study, based on a sample of 4000 subjects (see Table 3), to examine the correlation between major demographic characteristics and ownership or non-ownership of a dog. With certain reservations in respect of age, we were able to demonstrate the very limited explanation value of so-called demographic characteristics – which came as no surprise in the light of recent research findings (Bergler, 1982). Since age did appear to be a factor of some significance, we chose to carry out a supplementary psychological study focusing on the theme of 'dogs and the elderly'.

At this point it was thought advisable to subject the data of the primary study (see Chapter 6) to further analysis. Hitherto 'dog owners' had been treated as a homogeneous group, and comparisons with other groups were made on the basis of mean values. But it was also apparent, from the distribution of the findings, that dog owners could be divided into a number of distinct 'types'. In other words, the specific quality of the man–dog relationship is not the same for all dog owners. People differ both in terms of the extent to which a dog is capable of fulfilling personal aspirations and ideals, and in terms of the extent to which they must accept certain disadvantages as the price of that fulfilment. There are different types of dog owners: they differ in the quality of their psychological evaluation of dog ownership – and hence, of course, in their scores for dog ownership.

Age as a factor in dog ownership

In our critical analysis of the scientific literature in this field (see Chapter 5) it became clear that a dog might have an important function in the development of human behaviour. If we compare the role of a dog in the development of a child or adolescent with its role in the fulfilment of an elderly person, we can readily identify a number of age-specific aspects. Older dog owners frequently expect different things from a dog than younger owners. This is due in part to psychological differences in the social situation of the various age groups. The life situation of older persons is often characterized by failing health, the comparative or total absence of social and mental stimulation – and in many cases a sense of no longer being needed.

This has a significant impact on a person's independence, self-esteem and self-confidence, producing a sense of impaired quality of life and well-being. The social situation of young people is entirely different in this respect.

From a psychological point of view, of course, it would make much more sense to group people according to the quality of their social situation – isolation versus integration, quality of social stimulation or frustration, etc. More effectively than any conventional grouping by age, a psychological typology of this sort would undoubtedly serve better to highlight the function and significance of a dog under a multiplicity of social, ecological and health-related conditions. The conventional analysis offered here certainly furnishes a number of valuable insights, but it remains less than totally satisfactory as a contribution to developmental psychology. With that proviso, however, an analysis on the basis of age groups does yield some very telling findings in terms of what aspects of dog ownership are valued at what stage of life.

The special meaning and value a dog has for a person – and indeed his perception of the disadvantages it may bring – do change with the passing years, even though the dog in its function as 'sociable companion' is regarded as equally desirable by all, irrespective of age. For young persons in the 14–19 years age group, a dog is essentially a playmate, someone to cuddle. As a person gets older, this aspect diminishes in importance, to be superseded by other considerations – such as the need for regular daily exercise and a structured daily routine, plus a desire for order and responsibility.

The differences between the various age groups are also very apparent when we come to examine the cost factors of dog ownership. Up until retirement age, the aspects that give most cause for concern are the restrictions on personal freedom of movement imposed by a dog – and the additional expense and effort involved in making suitable alternative arrangements for looking after the animal. After retirement, however, these problems cease to loom so large. Instead, dog owners start to worry about what will happen to their dog if they fall ill or die. The positive contribution of a dog to personal quality of life at a time when people are frequently on their own is freely acknowledged, but this must be offset against the relatively high probability that the dog will also become a source of nuisance. Hence the general tendency for scores to fall slightly with advancing years. Conversely, as people get older they become less concerned about possible problems with neighbours and other residents, or about the need to compromise on their standards of domestic hygiene.

In order to define more closely what a dog means to the elderly, we shall carry out a series of comparisons between dog owners over the age of 60 and their juniors. We shall also be comparing elderly dog owners with elderly non-owners, putting forward a number of hypotheses that require some further verification.

Firstly, dog owners and non-owners alike are both agreed that a dog is perfectly capable of exercising a positive influence on one's personal well-being and contentment. Invited to give examples, subjects spontaneously mentioned the following benefits of a dog:

- helps to alleviate loneliness;
- forces a person to go for walks; gets a person out in the fresh air; good for the health;
- is a source of fun and enjoyment;
- gives a person a responsibility, something to do;
- is faithful, never lets you down;
- friendship, companionship;
- protects you; is vigilant;
- helps you to make new friends;
- introduces order into the daily routine: you have to stick to a certain 'timetable';
- wins respect and acknowledgement from other people;
- is obedient; a dog can be trained;
- is grateful.

The specific significance and value of a dog for the elderly is embodied in the following individual findings:

- The aspirations and values of the elderly are not the same as those of younger people. The energies of the young are primarily directed towards the cultivation of their personal and sexual relationships, the creation of a circle of friends, the safeguarding of their own independence and freedom of movement, and the upbringing of their children. This is not the case with the elderly, who are much more concerned with creating an orderly and stable environment. Their priorities tend to centre on the home, a well-ordered daily routine, freedom from stress, and proper provision in the event of their own illness or death. Quite clearly, therefore, well-being and quality of life are to some extent determined by the satisfaction of *age-specific* need structures.

- A number of benefit factors associated with dog ownership have a higher probability of occurrence for older persons than they do for the young. This applies particularly to the health-related benefits of dog ownership, which virtually forces a person to remain active, organize his day properly and stay in touch with nature. By and large, an active and well-regulated daily routine of this kind approximates to the ideal life-style for elderly dog owners. The only drawback they see is a certain restriction in their freedom of movement, compared with other people of their age who do not keep pets. However, such restrictions pale into insignificance compared with the benefits of health and fitness and the psychological gains in terms of responsibility and social interaction.

Elderly people without pets have a different set of priorities. They are more interested in mobility and sociability, enjoying outings to pubs and restaurants and walks in the city – and they also have a greater appetite for the media, including television and reading. But elderly persons who do own a dog tend to be more healthy, less lonely, and generally more contented with life.

- With regard to the probable cost factors of dog ownership, there are certain differences between the elderly and younger age groups in so far as younger dog owners tend to be more concerned about restrictions on their personal freedom of choice (e.g. when making holiday plans) and the financial cost of dog ownership. Older people, on the other hand, are more worried about what will happen to their dog if they fall ill or die. As one gets older, it seems, one becomes more aware of the dependency of animals upon humans – which in turn affects one's general attitude to pets, as reflected (for example) in their psychological scores. In this connection it is interesting to note that people without pets become increasingly negative in their attitudes to dog ownership as they grow older. In other words, it becomes more and more difficult to establish a positive relationship between man and dog, despite the psychological arguments in favour of it. An elderly person who does not own a dog is very unlikely to perceive a dog as something intrinsically desirable and attractive; the only merit he can see in a dog is as a means of personal protection. His whole attitude to dog ownership is characterized by over-simplification and negative stereotyping.

- The negative preconceptions that dog owners harbour about non-owners are more pronounced in elderly dog owners than in their younger counterparts. In other words, learned prejudices do not simply survive the passage of the years: they actually become stronger as a person grows older.

- The special quality of the man–dog relationship for elderly people can also be seen in the way they come to terms with some of the probable disadvantages of dog ownership. Table 28 contains a selection of verbatim answers to specific questions, and these show the ability and readiness of elderly people to adjust to possible negative aspects of dog ownership. Elderly non-owners, on the other hand, are unwilling or unable to adjust to these anticipated nuisance factors. The only potential problem thought 'unlikely to occur' by non-owners as well as owners is the transmission of diseases via a dog.

- The significance of a dog for one's own well-being – taking into account such demographic variables as age, sex, marital status (single, married, widowed, divorced), income, standard of education – is determined not only by one's age, but also by the circumstance of living alone, living with a partner, or living with a partner and children.

Table 28   Coming to terms with possible disadvantages of dog ownership

(List of standard questions put to subjects with dog; multiple replies possible)

Lack of independence:

- '. . . that doesn't really apply to me, I'm at home most of the time anyway; it doesn't happen very often . . .'
- '. . . you can always leave the dog at home for short periods, while you go and fetch something, if the dog can't come with you it's really no problem; I could leave him on his own and it wouldn't matter, he doesn't bark – I just prefer not to . . .'

Expenditure of time:

- '. . . I've got time on my hands; it doesn't bother me at all that I have to spend time on the dog, I don't have a lot else to do any more, I could

Table 28 *contd.*

even spend more time if it was necessary; now that I'm retired I don't mind having to attend to the dog – in fact I'm pleased to have something to do . . .'

- '. . . of course it demands a certain amount of time, but it's time well spent, it's a form of relaxation for me; the dog takes up time, but it all depends on whether it gives you pleasure or not . . .'

Financial costs:

- '. . . of course a dog costs money, but I don't begrudge spending it; obviously the licence and the food cost money, but there are plenty of things that cost more money – and don't give you half as much pleasure . . .'
- '. . . I'd say it was reasonable. Other people have their hobbies, after all – and they might cost a lot more money . . .'

Dirt:

- '. . . no, he's properly house-trained; my dog is completely clean, he doesn't make any mess; dogs aren't all that dirty . . .'
- '. . . when it's raining he brings a bit of mud into the house, of course, but it's not that bad; there's bound to be a bit of dirt, you can't teach a dog to wipe its feet or take its shoes off indoors, but that's the only thing, otherwise a properly trained dog is very clean; yes, the dog makes a bit of a mess, but then so do children – and any house needs regular cleaning anyway . . .'
- '. . . you can control it by teaching the dog what to do; if you arrange things properly a dog doesn't make a mess. Our dog has his own special rug under the table, where he likes to lie; we put a blanket on the sofa for him . . .'

Transmission of diseases:

- '. . . dogs are vaccinated against disease . . .'
- '. . . you have to take certain hygienic precautions, of course; you have to make sure you wash your hands fairly frequently; you simply mustn't let the dog lick you . . .'

Excessive noise:

- '. . . our dog barks when somebody comes, I think that's only natural, and I don't try to stop him; it's not excessive, he doesn't bark indoors, only outside, when he sees another dog, for example . . .'
- '. . . my dog is not especially noisy; he doesn't disturb anybody with his barking; my dog never makes too much noise, nobody has ever complained . . .'

Table 28 *contd.*

- '. . . it's all a matter of training, a well-trained dog doesn't yap and yelp. If he barks normally, there's nothing wrong with that . . .'

Trouble with the neighbours or landlord:

- '. . . I've never had any trouble of that sort; I've never had the slightest trouble with anyone. All the neighbours like my dog . . .'
- '. . . it's just a matter of common sense, learning to avoid trouble or sort it out afterwards. You just have to go along and apologize; you can't help it if a dog barks, but the neighbours are usually quite understanding . . .'

Disagreements with marital partner:

- '. . . in a healthy marriage you don't fall out over a dog; there's no argument between us, we both share the same views . . .'
- '. . . because we're both equally fond of the dog there's no jealousy or quarrel between us . . .'

Problems in case of illness or death:

- '. . . there's always somebody to take care of the dog, when I had my gall bladder operation a little while ago I was in the hospital for six weeks, and I left the dog with the children; if I die before he's reached the age of nine he won't be put to sleep, he'll go to some friends of mine – it's all in my will . . .'
- '. . . I'm not that old, and I'm not what you'd call ill; I haven't had to think about it so far, but it may be a problem as one gets older or falls ill . . .'

Typology of dog owners

The sheer diversity of human behaviour leads us to suppose that dog owners are a far from homogeneous group. For this reason we carried out a further analysis based on the psychological evaluation of dog ownership. This consisted of three stages:

1. Definition of groups (types) of dog owners on the basis of personal values.
2. Definition of groups (types) of dog owners in terms of how far a dog has specific advantages for them.
3. Definition of groups (types) of dog owners in terms of how far a dog has specific disadvantages for them.

In so-called grouping analyses (Rolett and Bertram, 1976), subjects are grouped together as 'types' if they show a minimum of deviation in their shared evaluation of the significance of certain factors – in this case, the benefits and costs of dog ownership. As a group, they also share a maximum of deviation from other groups. Put more simply, the differences between dog owners in any given group are as small as possible, while the differences between groups are as large as possible. With the aid of the chosen statistical qualitatively different attitude and value systems – or motivational states – with regard to a dog. It is not possible to classify every single dog owner in this way, of course. Out of our total of 345 dog owners, for example, only 223 can be assigned unequivocally to the three groups or 'types' which were defined with reference to the personal significance of certain specific values.

Figure 29 charts the personal significance of various factors for each of the three groups or types of dog owner. The three types may be characterized as follows:

Type I (n = 22): the independent type

This is someone who values his personal independence and mobility, who also likes to be relatively independent of other people, does not necessarily expect protection or gratitude, and does not give much thought to what will happen if he is ill or no longer there.

Type II (n = 57): the easy-going type

This type is characterized by a relative indifference to independence and the affection of others. He adapts more easily to changes in circumstance, and is less dependent on the recognition and respect of others. He is also less concerned about hygiene and cleanliness in the home.

Type III (n = 144): the responsible, well-adjusted type

Dog owners in this group attach great importance to most of the aspirations and values that dog ownership is thought to promote – except that child-rearing is widely perceived as a *personal* responsibility with which others cannot assist. This type represents a positive 'Mr. Average' – the kind of person who values all the things that make for socially desirable behaviour in our society.

It is clear, from these three profiles, that only Type I persons are

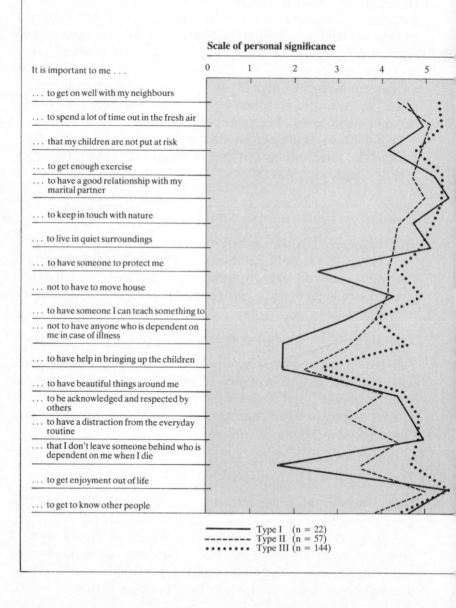

Fig. 29 Personal significance of needs associated with dog ownership (mean values) cluster analysis of dog-owner types

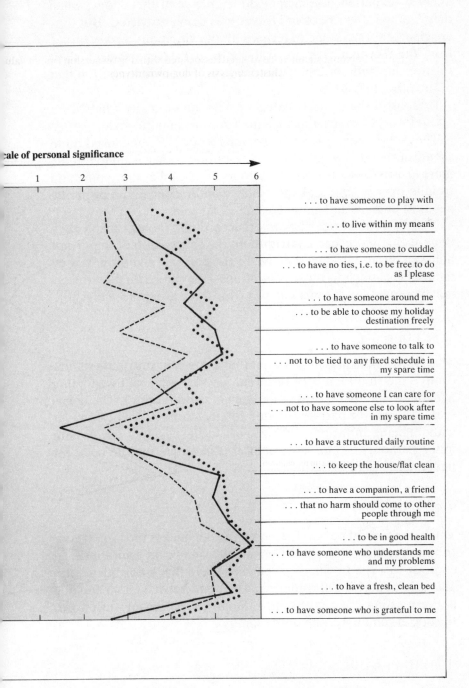

Scale of personal significance

| 1 | 2 | 3 | 4 | 5 | 6 |

. . . to have someone to play with

. . . to live within my means

. . . to have someone to cuddle

. . . to have no ties, i.e. to be free to do as I please

. . . to have someone around me

. . . to be able to choose my holiday destination freely

. . . to have someone to talk to

. . . not to be tied to any fixed schedule in my spare time

. . . to have someone I can care for

. . . not to have someone else to look after in my spare time

. . . to have a structured daily routine

. . . to keep the house/flat clean

. . . to have a companion, a friend

. . . that no harm should come to other people through me

. . . to be in good health

. . . to have someone who understands me and my problems

. . . to have a fresh, clean bed

. . . to have someone who is grateful to me

likely to experience recurrent difficulties with their dogs, when they feel that their personal freedom is being restricted. But they are clearly able to come to terms with this situation – as we can see from the fact that they are still dog owners. Nevertheless, their relationship with their pet is somewhat different in kind from that of the other two groups.

Persons in the Type II category have no difficulty whatsoever about incorporating a dog into their routine and life-style.

The well-being of Type III persons is certainly enhanced quite significantly by a dog, but this type of dog owner is undoubtedly more sensitive towards his pet and its needs, takes more time and trouble over it, and seeks to balance and reconcile the disparate needs of humans and animals.

If we now categorize dog owners according to how probable they think it that a dog can contribute to the satisfaction of important human aspirations – irrespective of the personal significance they themselves attach to those aspirations – we can again discern certain typological differences between the three groups (see Fig. 30).

Type I (n = 106)

This type of person is in no doubt that a dog can contribute significantly, and in all kinds of different ways, to personal well-being and quality of life (except in the area of child-rearing). The dog is seen as a genuine partner, related totally to one's own person, yet without being anthropomorphized in a facile, negative way. Where a dog is thought to be least helpful is in answering the need for understanding and gratitude.

Type II (n = 65)

This is the type of person for whom the dog makes the largest contribution to the fulfilment of personally significant aspirations. In contrast to Type I owners, Type IIs believe that a dog has a valuable role to play in child-rearing. The bond between man and dog is a very strong one, they live together in close intimacy – in a word, the dog is genuinely 'one of the family'.

Type III (n = 50)

These are people who tend to believe that a dog is able to satisfy real human needs only to a fairly limited extent. While Type III people certainly derive pleasure from dog ownership, a close and

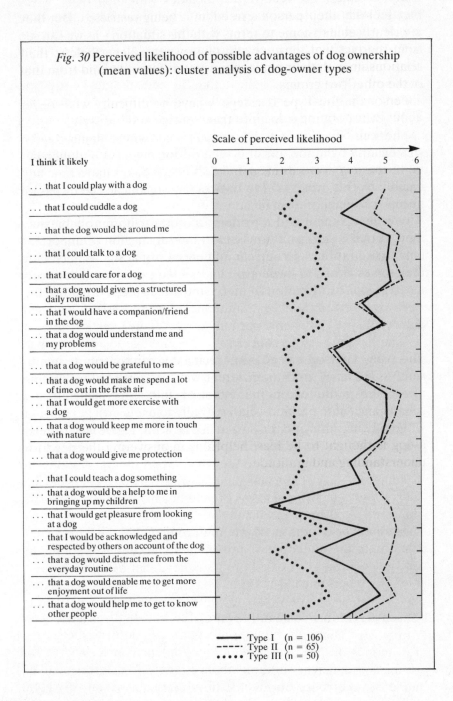

Fig. 30 Perceived likelihood of possible advantages of dog ownership (mean values): cluster analysis of dog-owner types

Scale of perceived likelihood

I think it likely

... that I could play with a dog

... that I could cuddle a dog

... that the dog would be around me

... that I could talk to a dog

... that I could care for a dog

... that a dog would give me a structured daily routine

... that I would have a companion/friend in the dog

... that a dog would understand me and my problems

... that a dog would be grateful to me

... that a dog would make me spend a lot of time out in the fresh air

... that I would get more exercise with a dog

... that a dog would keep me more in touch with nature

... that a dog would give me protection

... that I could teach a dog something

... that a dog would be a help to me in bringing up my children

... that I would get pleasure from looking at a dog

... that I would be acknowledged and respected by others on account of the dog

... that a dog would distract me from the everyday routine

... that a dog would enable me to get more enjoyment out of life

... that a dog would help me to get to know other people

——— Type I   (n = 106)
- - - - Type II   (n = 65)
• • • • Type III (n = 50)

intimate rapport between 'dog and master' does not develop. Even though such people quite like having the dog around, and occasionally feel the need to interact with it, there is not sufficient interest to cultivate an intensive relationship with the dog, to spend time training and teaching it or to arrange one's leisure time around it. These people believe that the animal must be subordinated to their own personal needs, and that a dog therefore has only limited potential as an alternative means of satisfying human aspirations. The dog does not occupy a central place as an object of gratification, and the owner does not form a constant attachment to it; the dog elicits interest and indifference in roughly the same measure. This group of dog owners is the one least given to 'anthropomorphizing' dogs in a positive sense.

We have established that there are clear differences between dog owners in terms of how important dogs are for them. Naturally, this in turn has a certain influence on the way they behave. The majority of dog owners are undoubtedly convinced that a dog has a major contribution to make to their own enjoyment of life, their own self-confidence – and hence their self-esteem and self-image. Where this is only partially the case, the question arises as to whether the persons concerned are spending too little time with their dog, viewing it as a kind of incidental amusement, to be pursued as the fancy takes them. And it may very well be that they are prevented, by this emotional instability, from appreciating the full significance of the relationship between man and dog.

Finally, we analysed the data to see how far dog owners differed with regard to the expected likelihood of disadvantages arising from dog ownership – i.e. to see what 'types' emerged under this heading (see Fig. 31). A first glance shows that dog owners fall into one of *four* categories in terms of their negative expectations – i.e. they tend to be more specific in their critical attitudes.

Here are brief profiles of the four groups:

Type I (n = 22)

These persons are constantly aware of certain disadvantages of dog ownership. These are thought most likely to occur in the form of restrictions on personal mobility and independence, and certain conflicts with neighbours and other residents. The perceived likelihood of occurrence of possible disadvantages is relatively great, with the result that scores for overall evaluation of dog ownership are not particularly positive. For these persons, a dog is capable of

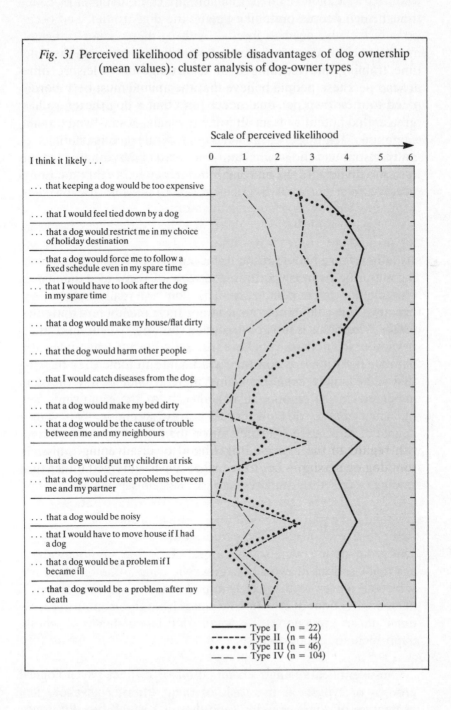

Fig. 31 Perceived likelihood of possible disadvantages of dog ownership (mean values): cluster analysis of dog-owner types

Scale of perceived likelihood

I think it likely . . .

0 1 2 3 4 5 6

. . . that keeping a dog would be too expensive

. . . that I would feel tied down by a dog

. . . that a dog would restrict me in my choice of holiday destination

. . . that a dog would force me to follow a fixed schedule even in my spare time

. . . that I would have to look after the dog in my spare time

. . . that a dog would make my house/flat dirty

. . . that the dog would harm other people

. . . that I would catch diseases from the dog

. . . that a dog would make my bed dirty

. . . that a dog would be the cause of trouble between me and my neighbours

. . . that a dog would put my children at risk

. . . that a dog would create problems between me and my partner

. . . that a dog would be noisy

. . . that I would have to move house if I had a dog

. . . that a dog would be a problem if I became ill

. . . that a dog would be a problem after my death

—————— Type I   (n = 22)
- - - - - - Type II (n = 44)
• • • • • • Type III (n = 46)
— — — — Type IV (n = 104)

fulfilling human needs only to a limited extent, while at the same time bringing many problems with it.

Type II (n = 44)

These people are similar in many ways to the Type III owners described below, but they differ from them in that they see a greater likelihood of conflict with the neighbours, while at the same time feeling less burdened overall by the possible duties, ties and constraints of dog ownership – not least in the planning of their leisure activities. In the final analysis their affection for their dog is hardly affected at all by their perception of possible drawbacks.

Type III (n = 46)

Although these people recognize a number of possible disadvantages to dog ownership, they see none of them as a significant obstacle for them personally. They do not really believe, for example, that a dog would harm strangers or members of their own family, or be a source of conflict between them and their neighbours. Nor do they believe that a dog poses a personal health hazard. If for any reason they are unable to look after the dog themselves, they cannot imagine there would be any problem about making alternative arrangements. At the same time they recognize that as dog owners they must accept – albeit with a degree of reluctance – restrictions on their own freedom of movement in the broadest sense, together with certain compromises in the area of domestic hygiene. Although basically well-disposed towards a dog, they are also critical of certain aspects.

Type IV (n = 104):

This group of dog owners – the largest of the four – is not aware of any really serious drawbacks to dog ownership, although there are some references to the restrictions that a dog imposes on one's personal freedom of movement. Apart from these minor reservations, these are people for whom dog ownership is a wholly unproblematic experience.

Our identification and examination of distinct psychological groups, or types, on the basis of their differing psychological evaluation of dog ownership (and there is virtually no difference between them in terms of demographic characteristics – age, occu-

pation, education, family status, income, etc.) enables us to summarize the position as follows:

The majority of dog owners view their dog as a genuine partner
and member of the family. Dogs are an accepted part of man's
environment, they belong to the world of human aspiration and
experience – and they help to enhance our enjoyment of life and
enrich our life-style.

The possible disadvantages of dog ownership are viewed more
critically than the possible advantages. Leaving aside those people
for whom a dog is capable of satisfying their needs and aspirations only to a limited degree, and who are constantly aware of the
problems associated with dog ownership, the remaining majority
of dog owners – who see their pets as an important positive influence on their quality of life – exhibit diverse critical attitudes to dog
ownership. These range from a wholly unproblematic view of dog
ownership to a perception of the difficulties that a dog can create
with neighbours and other residents – and the restrictions it can
impose on one's leisure activities. Each individual dog owner has
to come to terms with this in his own way, through a process of
learning that is undoubtedly facilitated by the pleasure that his dog
affords him.

Concluding remarks

We hope that this study has succeeded in demonstrating the inherent complexity of the two-way relationship between man and dog. As our fellow living creatures, dogs are clearly an integral part of our patterns of social interaction and our processes of communication. Dogs are judged and esteemed like all other living creatures, and are capable of contributing significantly to human well-being and quality of life. At the same time – again, in common with all other living creatures – they are naturally entitled to expect something in return from the environment they inhabit – which is to say, from man. Without mutual consideration, social life is neither possible nor desirable – and this applies no less to our association with animals than with our fellow human beings.

Appendix

Ideally, the publication of any scientific study should be accompanied, in the interests of reproducibility and repeatability, by a detailed account of the methods used to collect data (exploratory principles, questionnaires), full results of all supplementary analyses, and all relevant statistical indicators. In the case of the present study this would include all factor analyses of the various subject groups (dog owners, owners of other pets, non pet owners, positive/negative evaluation of dog ownership, etc.), analysis of data by age, sex and social status, values for 'practical significance', individual results of cluster analyses, etc. Regrettably, however, the sheer volume of these data – all of which were collected and processed for the present study* – makes this quite impossible. The notes which appear below are therefore designed simply to explain and amplify one or two salient points of methodology and procedure.

Heinz-Günter Hoff and the concept of 'practical significance'

'Practical significance' is an index value for the relative magnitude of a discovered effect (Bredenkamp, 1970). In addition to the standard determination of significance (which simply tells us, by means of pre-defined criteria, *whether* the manipulation of a particular experimental variable has had any measurable effect), we also get an index value telling us *how large* that effect has been. The index value for practical significance indicates how much of the total variance is attributable to manipulation of the experimental variables. A further important advantage of being able to specify a value for practical significance is that the latter is not dependent on the size of the sample. It is of course axiomatic that conventional 'significant' values are easier to obtain with a larger sample than a smaller one.

*I should like to acknowledge here the efforts of my colleague, Dr. Heinz-Günter Hoff, who laboured tirelessly to meet all my requests for computerized analysis of the study data. I am extremely grateful to him for the work he did on my behalf – and I must ask his indulgence for the fact that only a small portion of that work is reproduced in these pages.

In the case of studies that are not based on interval-scaled data, and which therefore cannot be subjected to a parametric analysis of variance, other criteria can be used to fulfil a similar function,

Table 32   Probability of occurrence of advantages of dog ownership

Analysis of differences between subject subgroups	Significance	Established variance (%)
I think it likely . . .		
. . . that I could play with a dog	< .000	6.9
. . . that I could cuddle a dog	< .000	5.5
. . . that the dog would be around me	< .000	9.0
. . . that I could talk to a dog	< .000	8.5
. . . that I could care for a dog	< .000	7.0
. . . that a dog would give me a structured daily routine	< .000	4.3
. . . that I would have a companion/ friend in the dog	< .000	6.1
. . . that a dog would understand me and my problems	< .000	3.3
. . . that a dog would be grateful to me	< .000	2.2
. . . that a dog would make me spend a lot of time out in the fresh air	< .000	2.2
. . . that I would get more exercise with a dog	< .000	2.0
. . . that a dog would keep me more in touch with nature	< .000	3.7
. . . that a dog would give me protection	< .05	0.7
. . . that I could teach a dog something	< .000	2.3
. . . that a dog would be a help to me in bringing up my children	< .000	1.9
. . . that I would get pleasure from looking at a dog	< .000	9.0
. . . that I would be acknowledged and respected by others on account of the dog	< .000	3.7
. . . that a dog would distract me from the monotony of everyday routine	< .000	7.2
. . . that a dog would enable me to get more enjoyment out of life	< .000	10.2
. . . that a dog would help me to get to know other people	< .000	2.8

i.e. give an indication of the strength or magnitude of a certain effect. Suitable criteria include coefficients of correlation, coefficients of contingency or coefficients of association (Bredenkamp, 1970; Clauss and Ebner, 1968).

Table 33 Probability of occurrence of disadvantages of dog ownership

Analysis of differences between subject subgroups	Significance	Established variance (%)
I think it likely . . .		
. . . that keeping a dog would be too expensive	< .000	7.9
. . . that I would feel tied down by a dog	< .000	16.7
. . . that a dog would restrict me in my choice of holiday destination	< .000	13.0
. . . that a dog would force me to follow a fixed schedule even in my spare time	< .000	10.9
. . . that I would have to look after the dog in my spare time	< .000	6.4
. . . that a dog would make my house/flat dirty	< .000	7.8
. . . that the dog would harm other people	< .000	9.1
. . . that I would catch diseases from the dog	< .000	9.5
. . . that a dog would make my bed dirty	< .000	6.8
. . . that a dog would cause trouble between me and my neighbours	< .000	8.1
. . . that a dog would put my children at risk	< .000	5.6
. . . that a dog would create problems between me and my partner	< .000	7.1
. . . that a dog would be noisy	< .000	8.8
. . . that I would have to move house if I had a dog	< .000	9.8
. . . that a dog would be a problem if I became ill	< .000	7.8
. . . that a dog would be a problem after my death	< .000	6.6

Table 34 Stereotype of the typical dog owner

Analysis of differences between subjects with positive scores and subjects with negative scores

Variables	N	chi²	sign.	V	tau-C	eta	r	AV	K	C
V123	917	70.26	.0001	0.28	−0.29	0.25	−0.25	6.25%	0.28	0.27
V124	915	128.74	.0001	0.38	−0.35	0.31	−0.31	9.8%	0.38	0.35
V125	913	56.80	.0001	0.25	+0.27	0.24	0.24	5.9%	0.25	0.24
V126	918	111.02	.0001	0.35	−0.36	0.31	−0.31	9.6%	0.35	0.33
V127	916	116.70	.0001	0.36	−0.38	0.34	−0.34	11.8%	0.36	0.34
V128	912	97.83	.0001	0.33	−0.32	0.29	−0.29	8.2%	0.33	0.31
V129	915	43.09	.0001	0.22	0.20	0.17	0.17	2.9%	0.22	0.21
V130	916	114.47	.0001	0.35	−0.37	0.33	−0.33	10.8%	0.35	0.33
V131	915	94.27	.0001	0.32	−0.34	0.32	−0.32	10.6%	0.32	0.31
V132	915	43.58	.0001	0.22	+0.21	0.20	0.20	3.9%	0.22	0.21
V133	916	102.98	.0001	0.34	0.30	0.29	0.29	8.3%	0.34	0.32
V134	914	55.23	.0001	0.25	−0.27	0.24	−0.24	6.0%	0.25	0.24
V135	917	89.23	.0001	0.31	−0.33	0.30	−0.30	9.1%	0.31	0.30
V136	912	108.70	.0001	0.35	+0.37	0.34	−0.34	11.4%	0.35	0.33
V137	916	64.83	.0001	0.27	−0.27	0.24	−0.24	6.0%	0.27	0.26

Evaluation of dog ownership: method of calculating scores

$$B = \frac{1}{n} \sum_{i=1}^{n} (w_i \cdot p_i) - \frac{1}{m} \sum_{j=1}^{m} (w_j \cdot q_j)$$

where

B   : score value (range: from -48 to $+48$)

w_i : subjective significance of value i (range: 1–7)

p_i : perceived likelihood of advantage i (range: 1–7)

i   : index of advantages

n   : number of advantages

w_j : subjective significance of value j (range: 1–7)

q_j : perceived likelihood of disadvantage j (range: 1–7)

j   : index of disadvantages

m   : number of disadvantages

This formula produces scores ranging between -48 and $+48$.

References

Ajzen, I. and Fishbein, M. (1977) 'Attitude-behavior-relations: A theoretical analysis and review of empirical research.' *Psychological Bulletin*, **84** 888–918.

Ajzen, I. and Fishbein, M. (1973) 'Attitudinal and normative variables as predictors of specific behavior.' *Journ. of Personality and Social Psychology*, **27** 41–57.

Ajzen, I. and Fishbein, M. (1970) 'The prediction of behavior from attitudinal and normative variables.' *Journ. of Experimental Social Psychology*, **6** 466–487.

Anderson, R.S. (Hg.) (1975) *Pet animals and society*. London: Bailliere Tindal.

Anderson, R.S. and Gantt, W.H. (1966) 'The effect of person on cardiac and motor responsivity to shock in dogs.' *Conditioned Reflex*, **1** 181–189.

Andrews, F.M. and Withey, S.B. (1976) *Social indicators of well-being*. New York: Plenum Press.

Andrysco, R.M. (1982) *A study of ethologic and therapeutic factors of pet-facilitated therapy in a requirement-nursing community*. Ohio State Univers.: Diss.

Argyle, M. (1972) *Soziale Interaktion*. Köln : Kiepenheuer u. Witsch.

Aschaffenburg, H. (1966) 'Jackie.' *Voices*, **2** 75–78.

Bath, M., Krook, A., Sandquist, G. and Stanze, K. (1976) *Is the dog needed? A study of the dog's social importance to man*. University of Gothenburg: Thesis.

Beck, A.M. (1975) 'The public health implications of urban dogs.' *American Journ. of Public Health*, **12** 1315–1318.

Bennett, R. (1973) 'Social isolation and isolation-reducing programs.' *Bulletin of the New York Academy of Medicine*, **12** 1143–1163.

Bergler, R. (1964). *Der typische Hundehalter*. Nürnberg: unveröff. Unters.

Bergler, R. (1965) *Die prinzipielle Mehrdimensionalität stereotyper Systeme – über qualitative und faktorielle Strukturen*. Wien: Ber. 24. Kongr. dt. Ges. f. Psych

Bergler, R. (1966) *Psychologie stereotyper Systeme*. Bonn, Stuttgart: Huber.

Bergler, R. (1974) *Sauberkeit, Norm, Verhalten, Persönlichkeit*. Bern, Stuttgart, Wien: Huber.

Bergler, R. (1975) *Das Eindrucksdifferential: Theorie und Technik.* Bonn, Stuttgart, Wien: Huber.

Bergler, R. (1979) 'Belastungen des Alterns.' *Therapie Woche,* **32** 4964–4972.

Bergler, R. (1981) 'Psychologie der Verwendung haarfärbender Produkte.' *Ärztliche Kosmetologie,* **2**.

Bergler, R. (1982) *Psychologie in Wirtschaft und Gesellschaft.* Köln: Dt. Inst. Verl.

Bergler, R. (1984) 'Risikofaktor Rauchen. Rauchermotivation und Raucherentwöhnung.' *Therapie Woche,* **34** 3787–3782.

Bergler, R. (erscheint 1986) *Attraktivität und Persönlichkeit.* Bonn, Stuttgart, Wien: Huber.

Bergler, R. (1987) Heimtierhaltung aus psychologischer Sicht. Zbl. Bakt. Hyg., I. Abt. Orig. (im Druck).

Bergler, R. and Six, U. (1979) *Psychologie des Fernsehens. Wirkungsmodelle und Wirkungseffekte unter besonderer Berücksichtigung der Wirkung auf Kinder und Jugendliche.* Bern, Stuttgart, Wien: Huber.

Bierhoff, H.W. (1973) 'Kosten und Belohnung: Eine Theorie sozialen Verhaltens.' *Zeitschrift für Sozialpsychologie,* **4** 297–317.

Bierhoff, H.W. (1974) 'Kognitive Repräsentanz von Verhaltensalternativen in ihrer Beziehung zu positiven und negativen Konsequenzen.' *Archiv für Psychologie,* **126** 131–146.

Blake, D.S. (1981) *On the introduction of pets for the institutionalized aging: An exploratory descriptive study of an intervention.* Columbia Univ. Teachers College: Diss.

Borcheld, P.L. (1983) 'Aggressive behavior of dogs kept as companion animals: Classification and influence of sex, reproductive status and breed.' *Applied Animal Ethology,* **10** 45–61.

Brandt, E.P. and Bower, P.J. (1975) 'Johnny's bird is dead and gone: Remedial work with a retarded pre-schooler.' *Canada's Mental Health,* **23** 19–20.

Bredenkamp, J. (1970) 'Über Maße der praktischen Signifikanz.' *Z. Psychol.,* **177** 309–318.

Brehm, J. and Cohen, A.R. (1962) *Explorations in cognitive dissonance.* New York: Wiley.

Brickel, C.M. (1979) 'The therapeutic roles of cat mascots with a hospital-based geriatric population. A stuff survey.' *The Gerontologist,* **19** 368–372.

Brickel, C.M. (1980/81). 'A review of the roles of pet animals in psychotherapy and with the elderly.' *Int. J. Aging and Human Development/Int. J. Aging,* **12** 119–128.

Brickel, C.M. (1982) 'Pet-facilitated psychotherapy: a theoretical explanation via attention shifts.' *Psychological Reports,* **50** 71–74.

Brown, L.T., Shaw, T.G. and Kirkland, K.D. (1972) 'Affection for people as a function of affection for dogs.' *Psychological Reports,* **31** 957–958.

Bühler, K. (1965) *Krise der Psychologie.* Stuttgart: Klett.

Cameron, P., Conrad, C., Kirkpatrick, D.B. and Bateen, R.J. (1966) 'Pet ownership and sex as determinants of stated affects toward others and estimates of others regard of self.' *Psychological Reports,* **19** 884–886.

Cameron, P. and Mattson, M. (1972) 'Psychological correlates of pet ownership.' *Psychological Reports,* **30** 286.

Clauss, G. and Ebner, H. (1968) *Grundlagen der Statistik für Psychologen, Pädagogen und Soziologen.* Berlin: VEB.

Corson, S.A. and Corson, E.O. (1978) 'Pets as mediators of therapy.' *Current Psychiatric Therapies,* 195–205.

Corson, S.A. and Corson, E.O. (1980) *Ethology & Nonverbal Communication in Mental Health.* Oxford, New York, Toronto, Sydney: Pergamon Press.

Corson, S.A. and Corson, E.O. (1980) 'Pet animals as nonverbal communication mediators in psychotherapy in institutional settings.' In: Corson, S.A. and Corson, E.O. (Ed.), *Ethology & Nonverbal Communication in Mental Health.* Oxford, New York, Toronto, Sydney: Pergamon Press.

Corson, S.A., Corson, E.O. and Gwynne, P.H. (1975) 'Pet-facilitated psychotherapy.' In: Anderson, R.S. (Ed.), *Pet animals and society,* London, 19–36: Bailliere Tindal.

Corson, S.A., Corson, E.O., Gwynne, P.H. and Arnold, E. (1975) 'Pet-facilitated psychotherapy in a hospital setting.' *Current Psychiatric Therapies,* 277–286.

Corson, S.A., Corson, E.O., Gwynne, P.H. and Arnold, L.E. (1977) 'Pet dogs as nonverbal communication links in hospital psychiatry.' *Comprehensive Psychiatry,* **18** 61–72.

Costa, T.T. Jr. and McCrae, R.R. (1980) 'Influence of extraversion and neuroticism on subjective well-being: happy and unhappy people.' *Journ. of Personality and Social Psychology,* **38** 668–678.

Crase, D.R. and Crase, D. (1976) 'Helping children understand death.' *Young Children,* **32** 21–25.

Cusack, O. and Smith, E. (1984) 'Pets and the elderly: The therapeutic bond.' *Activities, Adaption & Aging,* **4** 2–3.

De Viney, E., Dickert, J., Lockwood, R. (1983) 'The care of pets within child abusing families.' *International Journal for the Study of Animal Problems,* **4** 321–329.

De Fleur, M.L. and Westie, F.R. (1963) 'Attitude as a scientific concept.' *Social Forces,* **42** 17–31.

Delafield, G. (1975) *Self-perception and the effects of mobility training.* Univ. of Nottingham: Diss.

Doyle, M.C. (1976) 'Rabbit: therapeutic prescription.' *Perspectives in Psychiatric Care,* **13** 79–82.

Edwards, A.L. (1959) *Edwards personal preference test: schedule A*. New York: Psychological Corp.

Eysenck, H.J. and Eysenck, S.B. (1969) *Personality structure and measurement*. London.

Feather, N.T. (1982) 'Human values and the prediction of action: An expectancy-value analysis.' In Feather, N.T. (Ed.), *Expectations and action*.

Feddersen-Petersen, D. (1984) *Soziales Verhalten des Hundes/Die Sprache des Hundes*. Baden-Baden: Vortrag.

Festinger, L. (1942) 'A theoretical interpretation of shifts in level of aspiration.' *Psychological Review*, **49** 235–250.

Festinger, L. (1957) *A theory of cognitive dissonance*. Stanford: Stanford Univ. Press.

Fishbein, M. (1967) 'Attitude and the prediction of behavior.' In Fishbein, M. (Ed.), *Readings in attitude, theory and measurement*. New York: Wiley & Sons, Inc.

Fishbein, M. (1972) 'The search for attitudinal-behavior-consistency.' In Cohen, I.B. (Ed.), *Behavioral science foundation of consumer behavior*. New York.

Fishbein, M. and Ajzen, I. (1975) *Belief, attitude, intention, and behavior*, 477–492. Reading: Mass. Addison-Wesley Pub. Co.

Friedmann, E. (1983) *Heimtierhaltung und Überlebenschancen nach Herzkranzgefäß-Erkrankungen*. In Interessensgemeinschaft Dt. Hundehalter e. V. (Ed.), (1983) Hamburg.

Friedmann, E., Katcher, A.H., Thomas, S.A. and Lynch, J.J. (1983) 'Social interaction and blood pressure – Influence of animal companions.' *Journ. of Nervous and Mental Disease*, **171** 461–465.

Friedmann, M. and Roseman, R.H. (1975) *Der A-Typ und der B-Typ*. Hamburg: Rowohlt.

Frith, G.H. (1982) 'Pets for handicapped children: A source of pleasure, responsibility, and learning.' *Pointer*, **1** 24–27.

George, Lk. (1979) 'The happiness syndrome: Methodological and substantive issues in the study of socialpsychological well-being in adulthood.' *The Gerontologist*, **19** 210–216.

Goodwin, R.D. (1975) 'Trends in the ownership of domestic pets in Great Britain.' In Anderson, R.S. (Ed.), *Pet animals and society*. London: Bailliere Tindal.

Gough, H.G. and Heilbrun, A.B. (1965) *The adjective check list manual*. Palo Alto, C.A.: Consulting Psychologist Press.

Gross, St. J. and Niman, C.M. (1975) 'Attitude-behavior consistency: A review.' *The Public Opinion Quarterly*, **39** 358–368.

Harris, R.J. (1976) 'Handling negative inputs. On the plausible equity formulae.' *Journ. of Experimental Social Psychology*, **12** 194–209.

Heckhausen, H. (1977) 'Achievement motivation and its constructs: A cognitive model.' *Motivation and Emotion*, **4** 283–329.

Hirsch-Pasek, K. and Treiman, R. (1982) 'Doggerel: Motherese in a new context.' *Journal of Child Language,* **9** 229–237.Hogan, R. (1969) 'Development of an empathy scale.' *Journ. of Consulting and Clinical Psych.,* **33** 307–316.

Hyde, K.R., Kurdek, L. and Larson, P.C. (1969) 'Relationship between pet ownership and self-esteem, social sensitivity, and interpersonal trust.' *Psychological Report,* **52** 110.

Interessensgemeinschaft dt. Hundehalter e. V. (o. Jahresangabe). *Der Hund: Eine Dokumentation.* Hamburg.

Katcher, A. (1979) Social support: Effects of pet ownership. Int. Group for the Study of the Human/Companion Animal Bond (Ed.), University of Dundee: University of Dundee Press.

Katona, G. (1960a) *The powerful consumer.* New York, Toronto, London: McGraw-Hill Book Company, Inc.

Katona, G. (1960b) *Das Verhalten der Verbraucher und Unternehmer.* Tübingen: J.C.B. Mohr (Paul Siebeck).

Kaufmann, I. (1976) 'Haustiere im Erleben Zehnjähriger: Skizzierte Untersuchungser-gebnisse aus ländlichen Gegenden Ostwestfalen-Lippe.' *Praxis der Kinderpsychologie,* **26** 52–56.

Keddie, K.M. (1977) 'Pathological mourning after the death of a domestic pet.' *British Journ. of Psychiatry,* **131** 21–25.

Kidd, A.H. and Feldmann, B.M. (1981) 'Pet ownership and self-respection of older-people.' *Psychological Reports,* **48** 867–875.

Kidd, A.H., Kelly, H.T. and Kidd, R.M. (1983) 'Personality characteristics of horse, turtle, snake, and bird owners.' *Psychological Reports,* **52** 719–729.

Kidd, A.H. and Kidd, R.M. (1980) 'Personality-characteristics and preferences in pet ownership.' *Psychological Reports,* **46** 939–949.

Kluckhohn, C. (1965) 'Values and value orientation in the theory of action. An exploration in definition and classification.' In Parsons, T. and Shils, E.A. (Ed.), *Toward a general theory of action.* New York: Harper & Row.

Kusnetzoff, J.C. (1982) 'Un doberman en la transferencia.' *Revisita de Psicoanalisis,* **2/3** 369–385.

Lee, R. (1976) *The pet dog: interactive correlates of a man–animal relationship.* Univers. of Hull: Progress report. Dept. Psych.

Levinson, B.M. (1962) 'The dog as a "co-therapist".' *Mental Hygiene,* **46** 59–65.

Levinson, B.M. (1964) 'Pets: A special technique in child psychotherapy.' *Mental Hygiene,* **48** 243–248.

Levinson, B.M. (1965) 'The veterinarian and mental hygiene.' *Mental Hygiene,* **49** 320–323.

Levinson, B.M. (1969) 'Pets and old age.' *Mental Hygiene,* **3** 364–368.

Levinson, B.M. (1969a) *Pet-owned child psychotherapy.* Springfield: Charles C. Thomas.

Levinson, B.M. (1969b) 'The value of pets ownership.' *Proceedings of the 12th Annual Convention of the Pet Food Institute,* 12–18.

Levinson, B.M. (1970a) 'Pets, child development, and mental illness.' *Journ. of the American Veterinary Medical Association,* **157** 1759–1766.

Levinson, B.M. (1970b) *The pet in the nursing home: A psychological adventure for the patient.* Silver Threads.

Levinson, B.M. (1971) 'Household pets in training schools serving delinquent children.' *Psychological Reports,* **2** 475–481.

Levinson, B.M. (1972a) *Pets and human development.* Springfield: Charles C. Thomas.

Levinson, B.M. (1972b) 'Man, animal, nature.' *Modern Veterinarian Practice,* **4** 35–41.

Levinson, B.M. (1975) 'Pets and environment.' In Anderson, R.S. (Ed.), *Pets animals and society.* London: Bailliere Tindal.

Levinson, B.M. (1978) 'Pets and personality development.' *Psychological Reports,* **42** 1031–1038.

Levinson, B.M. (1980) 'The child and his pet: A world of nonverbal communication.' In Corson, S.A., Corson, E.O. (Ed.), *Ethology and Nonverbal Communication in Mental Health.* Oxford, New York, Toronto: Pergamon Press.

Levinson, B.M. (1982) 'The future of research into relationships between people and their animal companion.' *Intern. Journ. for the Study of Animal Problems,* **3** 283–294.

Lynch, J.J., Fregin, G.F., Mackie, J.B. and Monroe, R.R. (1974) 'The effect of human contact on the heart activity of horse.' *Psychology,* **11** 472–478.

Lynch, J.J. and McCarthy, J.F. (1969) 'Social responding in dogs: Heart rate changes to person.' *Psychology,* **5** 389–393.

Lynch, J.J. and McCarthy, J.F. (1977) 'The effect of petting on a classically conditioned emotional response. *Behavioral Research and Therapy,* **5** 55–62.

MAFO-Institut (1983) *Arzt und Hund.* Schwalbach (Ts): unveröff. Untersuchung.

MAFO-Institut (1984) *Einstellung zur Hundehaltung.* Schwalbach (Ts): unveröff. Untersuchung.

Mahon, E. and Simpson, D. (1977) 'The painted guinea pig.' *Psychoanalytic Study of the Child,* **32** 282–303.

Martinez, R.L. and Kidd, A.H. (1980) 'Two personality-characteristics in adult pet-owners and non-owners.' *Psychological Reports,* **47** 318.

Mayr, A. (1987) Experimentelle Untersuchungen über Hygiene in Haushalten mit Tieren. Zbl. Bakt. Hyg., I. Abt. Orig. (im Druck).

Mitchel, T.B. (1974) 'Expectancy models of job satisfaction, occupational preference and effort. A theoretical, methodological and empirical appraisal.' *Psychological Bulletin,* **12** 1053–1077.

Moscovici, S. (1979) *Sozialer Wandel durch Minoritäten.* München, Wien, Baltimore: Urban & Schwarzenberg.

Mugford, R.A. (1980) 'The social significance of pet ownership.' In Corson, S.A. Corson, E.O. (Ed.), *Ethology and Nonverbal Communication in Mental Health.* Oxford, New York, Toronto: Pergamon Press.

Mugford, R.A. and M'Comisky, J.G. (1975) 'Some recent works on the psychotherapeutic value of cage birds.' In Anderson, R.S. (Ed.), *Animals and Society.* London: Bailliere Tindal.

Murray, M.A. (1938) *Explorations in personality.* New York: Oxford Univ. Press.

Newton, J.E. and Ehrlich, W.W. (1966) 'Coronary blood flow in dogs: Effect of person.' *Conditioned Reflex,* **1** /-81.

O.V. (o. Jahresangabe). *Klein Bettlektüre für alle, deren Herz für einen Hund schlägt.* Scherz-Verlag.

Parsons, T. and Shils, E.A. (1965) *Toward a general theory of action.* New York: Harper & Row.

Pass, H. (1979) *Sozialpsychologie der Kaufsituation.* Bonn: Diplomarbeit.

Pervin, L.A. and Smith, S.H. (1968) 'Further tests of the relationship between satisfaction and perceived self-environment similarity.' *Perceptual and Motor Skills,* **26** 835–838.

Petermann, F. (1985) 'Zum Situationsbegriff in der Diagnostik – unter besonderer Berücksichtigung pädagogischer Anwendungsmöglichkeiten.' in Jäger, R.S., Horn, R. and Ingenkamp, K. (Ed.), *Tests und Trends. 4. Jahrbuch der pädagogischen Diagnostik.* Weinheim: Beltz.

Piotrowsky, W. (1984) *Der Hund als Medizin.* Universität Heidelberg: Klinikum Mannheim.

Quinn-Kevins, C. (1983) *Mixed vs. pure breed dogs: Reported personality characteristics of owners, their dogs, and reasons for ownership.* Univers. of Pennsylvania: Diss.

Rollet, B. and Bertram, M. (1976) *Einführung in die hierarchische Chlusteranalyse.* Stuttgart: Klett.

Rubin, H.D. and Beck, A.M. (1982) 'Ecological behavior of free-ranging urban pet dogs.' *Applied Animal Ethology,* **1/2** 161–168.

Ryan, M.J. and Bonfield, E.M. (1975) 'The Fishbein extended model and consumer behavior.' *Journ. of Consumer Research,* **2** 118–136.

Ryder, R.D. (1973) 'Pets in man's search for sanity.' *Journal of Small Animal Practice*, **14** 657–668.

Rynearson, E.K. (1978) 'Humans and pets and attachment.' *British Journal of Psychiatry*, **133** 550–555.

Salomon, A. (1982) 'Des enfants montrealais face au test des affinites animales.' *Animales Medico-Psychologigues*, **2** 207–224.

Schaefer, H. (1977) 'Epidemiologie der coronaren Herzkrankheiten.' In Blohmke, M., Färber, C.H., v. Kister, K.E., Schaefer, H. (Ed.), *Handbuch der Sozialmedizin*. Bd. 2.

Schmidtchen, G. (1984) *Neue Technik. Neue Arbeitsmoral*. Eine sozialpsychologische Untersuchung über die Motivation in der Metallindustrie. Köln: Deutscher Instituts-Verlag.

Schmitt, B.D. and Kempe, C.H. (1975) 'The pediatrician's role in child abuse and neglect.' *Current Problems in Pediatrics*, **5** 1–47.

Schultz, W.C. (1958) *FIRO: a three-dimensional theory of interpersonal behavior*. New York: Holt Rinehart & Winston.

Schwartz, S.H. (1973) 'Normative explanations of helping behavior: A critique proposal and empirical test.' *Journ. of Experimental Social Psychology*, **9** 349–364.

Serpell, J.A. (1981) 'Childhood pets and their influence on adult attitudes.' *Psychological Reports*, **49**, 651–654.

Sherick, I. (1981) 'The significance of pets for children: Illustrated by a latency-age girl's use of pets in her analysis.' *Psychoanalytic study of the Child*, **36**, 193–215.

Sheth, J.N. (1971). 'Affect, behavioural intention and buying behaviour as a function of evaluative beliefs.' In: Pellemans, P. (Ed.), *Insights in consumer and market behaviour*. Belgium: Namur.

Sheth, J.N. (1974) 'A field study of attitude structure and attitude-behavior-relationship.' In: Sheth, J.N. (Ed.), *Models of buyer behavior: conceptual, quantitative and empirical*. New York.

Siegel, A. (1964) 'The journal investigates: Pet therapy. An unlighted path.' *Journ. of Small Animal Practice*, **5**, 275–279.

Templer, D.I., Salter, C.A., Dickey, S. and Baldwin, R. (1981) 'The construction of a pet attitude scale.' *Psychological Records*, **31**, 343–348.

Teutsch, G.M. (1980) 'Kinder und Tiere: Von der Erziehung zu mitgeschöpflichem Verhalten.' *Unsere Jugend*, **32**, 435–455.

Thibaut, J.W. and Kelley, H.H. (1959) *The social psychology of groups*. New York: Wiley.

Thomae, H. (1983) 'Motivationsbegriffe und Motivationstheorien.' in Thomae, H. (Ed.), *Enzyklopädie der Psychologie. Theorien und Formen der Motivation*. Göttingen: Hogrefe.

...pson, M.K. (1973) 'Adaptions to loneliness in old age.' *Proceedings ...f the Royal Society of Medicine*, **66**, –887.

Thurlow, H.J. (1967) 'General susceptibility to illness: A selective review.' *Canadian Mental Association Journ.*, **97**, 1397–1404.

Tortora, D. (1978) 'Psycho-Tierapie.' *Psychologie Heute*, **5**, 56–64.

Überla, K. (1968) *Faktorenanalyse*. Berlin: Springer.

Vroom, V.H. (1964) *Work and motivation*. New York: Wiley.

Wahaba, M.A. and House, R.J. (1974). 'Expectancy theory in work and motivation: Some logical and methodological issues.' *Human Relations*, **2**, 121–147.

Walster, D. (1979) 'The role of pets in the mental health of the elderly.' Int. Group for the study of the Human/Companion animal bond (Ed.). Dundee: University of Dundee Press.

Weinert, A. (1981) *Lehrbuch der Organisationspsychologie*. München: Urban & Schwarzenberg.

Wicker, A.W. (1969) 'Attitudes versus actions: the relationship of verbal and overt behavioral response to attitude objects.' *Journ. of Social Issues*, **25**, 41–78.

Wilbur, R.H. (Ed), (4./5. 2. 1976) 'Pets, pet ownership and animal control: Social and psychological attitudes. In: Proceedings of the national conference on dog and cat contr. (1976). Denver, Colorado (1976).

Wilson, D.T., Mathews, H.L. and Harvey, J.W. (1975) 'An empirical test of the Fishbein behavioral intention model. *Journ. of Consumer Research*, **1/4**, 39–48.

Wolfe, J. (1977) *The use of pets as transitional objects in dolescent interpersonal functioning*. Univ. of Columbia: Diss.

Yoxall, A. and Yoxall, M. (1979) *The multi-disciplinary approach to problems arising from pet-owner relationships*. Int. Group for the study of the human/companion animal bond (Ed.), /. Dundee: University of Dundee Press.

Zemanek, M. (1981) *Motivation zur Heimtierhaltung*. Universität Wien: Dissertation.

Zimmermann, I. (1982) 'Haustiere – Medizin für kranke Herzen.' *TK-Mitgliederzeitschrift*, **9**, 14–15.